THE ULTIMATE BOSTON RED SOX
TIME MACHINE BOOK

THE ULTIMATE BOSTON RED SOX TIME MACHINE BOOK

MARTIN GITLIN

LYONS
PRESS

Guilford, Connecticut

An imprint of The Rowman & Littlefield Publishing Group, Inc.
4501 Forbes Blvd., Ste. 200
Lanham, MD 20706
www.rowman.com

Distributed by NATIONAL BOOK NETWORK

British Library Cataloguing in Publication Information available

Library of Congress Cataloging-in-Publication Data available

ISBN 978-1-4930-4584-6 (paperback)
ISBN 978-1-4930-4585-3 (e-book)

∞™ The paper used in this publication meets the minimum requirements of American National Standard for Information Sciences—Permanence of Paper for Printed Library Materials, ANSI/ NISO Z39.48-1992.

CONTENTS

INTRODUCTION

A FEELING OF MAGICAL ANTICIPATION WASHED OVER THIS 10-YEAR-OLD Cleveland kid on a warm June day in the summer of 1967.

Our family had stopped in Boston en route to Cape Cod, where we were to spend most of our annual vacation. The layover was purposeful—my beloved Indians were in town. It was, of course, the Impossible Dream season for the Red Sox, but only their most optimistic fans could have imagined a storied four-team pennant race from which Boston would emerge victorious. After all, both clubs arrived at the park that day playing around .500 ball.

"Look at this, dad!" I screeched in my annoying, high-pitched voice as Fenway came into view. "It's a ballpark you just walk right into from the street!"

Amazing indeed for a boy accustomed to trudging great distances to get to massive Municipal Stadium, whose placement on the shores of Lake Erie separated it gloomily from a city that had been losing its vibrancy. The contrast was striking. Fenway Park blended beautifully into the bustling Boston thoroughfares.

The differences grew more distinct upon arrival. One usually entered the cavernous ballpark in Cleveland to the sight of 75,000 empty seats. The field had grown shabby despite the efforts of grounds crews that, like putting lipstick on a pig, toiled in vain to mask the damage done by drainage problems and Cleveland Browns players churning up the grass. It featured little inside to differentiate itself from other mammoth baseball venues. No nooks, no crannies. One can understand why my first peek inside Fenway proved a sensory delight. The big crowd. The Green Monster. The Pesky Pole. The stands that jutted out past third base. The "triangle" in right-center. I delightfully soaked in each nuance.

A Red Sox fan was born that day. I would forever remain an Indians loyalist. The allegiance to my hometown team would never wane. But if the Indians couldn't win—and they never could until I had reached middle age in the mid-1990s—I always rooted for the Red Sox. I gained an appreciation for their history and yearned for them to finally earn a World Series crown. I embraced slugging teams (the hard-hitting Pirates of the 1970s became my National League favorite) and cozy Fenway always inspired the Red Sox organization to develop or trade for prolific hitters. Ruth (OK—don't go there). Williams. Yaz. Rice. Evans. Vaughn. Big Papi. Betts.

But Red Sox Nation understands that the greatness of the franchise extends far beyond the batsmen that pummeled the Monster or sent baseballs soaring over it or onto Lansdowne Street. Their history is more one akin to Captain Ahab and Moby Dick—the 86-year pursuit to end the Curse of the Bambino. It is one of triumph and tragedy. It is one of personalities both loved and despised. It is about decisions and judgments that resulted in tearful nights or championship parades. It is, as was famously expressed in the introduction to *Wide World of Sports*, about the thrill of victory and agony of defeat.

This is the story of the franchise from the time they were known as the Boston Americans to today. It's a story about players and eras that shaped perhaps the most colorful history of any team in Major League Baseball. It's a story about Red Sox Nation and events, players, and managers they remember fondly or miserably that jar those memories in a few words: the Curse, Splendid Splinter, The Impossible Dream, The Tragedy of Tony C., Rocket Roger, Buckner, Bucky Freaking Dent, Spaceman, Grady Little, The Comeback, Big Papi, Manny Being Manny. One and all contributed to the rollercoaster Boston fans have been riding for well over a century.

Reliving Red Sox history was certainly made easier since the Curse was broken in 2004. Heartache runs a distant second to joy in the battle of emotions, courtesy of four World Series championships. You can enjoy the *The Ultimate Boston Red Sox Time Machine Book* now that the mention of Bucky Dent or Bill Buckner can bring a sigh and a smile rather than frustration and anger.

CHAPTER ONE

Super Cy and the First Series Champs

THE MOST FAMOUS FICTIONAL BAR IN BOSTON MIGHT FOREVER BE Cheers, where everybody knows your name, especially that of Norm. But the most legendary actual watering hole in Beantown is arguably the Third Base Saloon on Columbus Avenue, where owner Michael T. McGreevy served booze to fellow baseball fans. McGreevy earned the colorful nickname "Nuf Ced" because his inevitable utterance of those misspelled words ended arguments between loyalists of the Americans, who eventually morphed into the Red Sox, and the Beaneaters, later known as the Braves.[1]

There was no argument regarding popularity around the turn of the 20th century. The Beaneaters finished last or second-last in National League attendance every season from 1901 to 1913. The soon-to-be-Sox outdrew them three to one despite the fledgling status of the American League and placed in its top half in attendance every year until the fateful 1919 season, after which Babe Ruth was sent packing to the Big Apple.

It comes as no surprise, then, that a cheering section organized by McGreevy would target the Americans rather than their crosstown counterparts. That group of strong-lunged patrons called the Royal Rooters had much to shout about. The Americans emerged immediately as a power in what became known as the junior circuit.

The Rooters frequented the Huntington Avenue Grounds, which opened in 1901 and boasted a capacity of about 11,500. Constructed on a defunct circus lot, the field was unique for its massive dimensions and challenging hindrances. Among them was a home-run distance to center

The Royal Rooters watch a foul ball at the Huntington Avenue Grounds during the 1903 World Series.

1900 portrait (clockwise from left) of Red Sox second baseman Bobby Lowe, first baseman Fred Tenney, shortstop Herman Long and third baseman Jimmy Collins.

field that extended a ridiculous 530 feet away from home plate in 1901. Rather than shortening it for the hitters, the powers-that-be sadistically increased it to 635 feet in 1908. Dead Ball Era, Live Ball Era, it wouldn't have mattered. The only home runs the Americans and their opponents hit in that direction were inside-the-park jobs. Such round-trippers were certainly possible—line drives that zipped between outfielders would roll forever. That is, unless they hit the unintentional sand traps that dotted the grassy expanses or the eyesore supply shed that stood deep in the outfield and was ridiculously deemed in-play.[2]

The Royal Rooters had plenty to root for upon the creation of the American League in 1901 as the team forged winning records in its first two seasons behind third baseman/manager Jimmy Collins, who revolutionized his defensive position by charging the plate when suspecting the bunt, bringing greater mobility to the spot. Fellow standouts included first baseman Buck Freeman, outfielder Patsy Dougherty, and ace-of-all-aces Denton "Cy" Young. But it was not until Young received mound assistance from fellow 20-game winners Bill Dinneen and Tom Hughes in 1903 that the Americans were transformed from mild contenders to the first World Series champions.[3]

That Young would remain viable enough to notch what will remain forever a history-best 511 victories seemed quite unlikely a few years earlier. The right-hander who had averaged 34 wins a season with Cleveland from 1891 to 1898 had lost the zip on a fastball later compared favorably to that of Walter "Big Train" Johnson. He had been transferred along with nearly all the top Cleveland talent to St. Louis in 1899 by Frank Robison, the unscrupulous owner of both teams. A rib injury caused his failure in 1900 to win more than 20 games for the first time in 10 seasons. So frustrated had Young become that he attacked a fan in the stands who accused him of quitting on the team.[4]

Young signed with the Americans in 1901 and proved, to mangle a line from Mark Twain, that reports of his career demise had been greatly exaggerated. The theory that Young was about to disprove had been promoted by Robison, who claimed the soon-to-be-34-year-old pitcher was all but washed up. The defection of Young would not have given the AL immediate credibility if his production continued to deteriorate. But the

Cy Young was arguably the greatest pitcher who ever graced a major league mound.
WIKIMEDIA COMMONS

aging right-hander responded with the best season of his career in 1901, winning 33 of 43 decisions and posting a league-best 1.62 earned run average. He won what is now known as the pitching Triple Crown by leading the American League in strikeouts as well. Nothing that Young did in 1902 led anyone to believe those numbers were a fluke or a final flicker before his career burned out. He paced the league that year with 32 victories and 43 complete games.

The claim of lost velocity had validity. But the wily Young remarkably *increased* his strikeout totals later in his career despite the loss of zip on his heater and a noticeable girth protruding from his midsection. The magic came in the form of two distinctly different curveballs, one overhand with a sharp break and the other sidearm with a sweeping arc. He even occasionally fired submarine style to throw off timing and cause right-handed hitters to bail out. Young improved the pinpoint control that allowed him to lead the American League in fewest walks per nine innings an incredible 14 times in his career. He had become a Rembrandt on the mound. He was a surefire Hall of Famer before he arrived in Boston but was now in the conversation as the greatest pitcher ever to grace a major-league mound.[5]

The nickname "Cy" that was short for "Cyclone" no longer applied as the fastball lost velocity. But there was good reason for legendary sportswriter Grantland Rice penning lyrical praise for Young, whose name would forever be etched not only into the record books, but to an annual award for pitching excellence that he would have captured often had it existed in his day. Offered Rice: "So when a stalwart steps out from the throng, On with the tribute, let garlands be flung, Here's to the sturdy and here's to the strong, Here's to the king of them all, Denton Young."[6]

The king of them all remained on his throne in 1903. But then, all the Boston stars twinkled that year. Many, in fact, shined their brightest. The list of virtual one-year wonders is startling:

- Coming off a brilliant rookie season in 1902, Dougherty led the league with 195 hits and batted .331. He would never bat over .289 again.

- Freeman had been among the premier sluggers in baseball since before the turn of the century. He batted .287 and drove in an AL-best 104 runs in 1903, then never thereafter approached that level of production.

- Shortstop Freddie Parent hit .304 with 83 runs and 80 RBIs in 1903. His stats weakened the following year before fading dramatically.

- The post-1903 curse apparently took time to affect Dinneen, who managed a 21-13 record and 2.26 ERA that year. He followed with another brilliant campaign in 1904, then began collapsing before turning 30.

- Starting pitcher Tom Hughes achieved his only 20-win campaign in 1903. He finished over .500 only twice more in 10 seasons, though he received little run support pitching for the perennial punching bag and weak-hitting Washington Senators.

The stars indeed aligned ideally for the Americans in 1903. And the organization was certainly smart to cater to Young. The team trained that spring in Macon, Georgia, where their ace was coaching the Mercer University baseball team. After all, major-league players worked year-round well beyond 1903 and Young reportedly earned an annual salary from the Americans of about $3,000.[7]

That spring training did not catapult Boston to immediate greatness. The team started slowly in the regular season, falling to 5-7 with a loss to the Philadelphia Athletics on May 2 and to 13-14 after back-to-back defeats to the lowly St. Louis Browns three weeks later. The Americans were fortunate that no foe had zoomed out to separate itself from the pack. They warmed with the weather, winning 13 of 14, including 11 in a row, to take over first place. They showed the potential of dominance during one eight-game stretch, outscoring their opponents 66–19.

Following a short period of mediocrity that pushed the Americans from the top, they regained the lead for good with a 1–0 defeat of Detroit on June 23. A 13-3 blitz through Independence Day that ended with the Americans four games up was marked by brilliant individual performances. In a win at Cleveland on June 21, Freeman became the first player in franchise history to hit for the cycle. The super staff hurled six of its league-high 20 shutouts during that stretch as well. Included were three successive complete-game 1–0 victories by Young, a feat that has since never been duplicated.[8]

So incredible was the rotation of Young, Dinneen, Hughes, and sometimes-starters Norwood Gibson and George Winter that a bullpen proved unnecessary. The quintet hurled every inning as either starters or relievers the entire season aside from one. That frame belonged to Nick Altrock, who was clobbered in a 10–3 loss to Chicago on June 30 and summarily dispatched to the same Sox two days later. He sought revenge in a matchup against the Americans on July 8 and was mashed again in a 6–1 defeat.

A two-team race emerged. The Athletics hung around into early August. They closed to within 2½ games of the Americans with a 4–3 win in Philadelphia. But Boston won the last game of that series, then swept their nearest competitor three straight, outscoring Philly 23–9 in the process with the Royal Rooters screaming support at the Huntington Avenue Grounds. That blitz pushed the lead to 6½ games. The Athletics never recovered. They lost 17 of their next 23 while the Americans took their momentum and ran with it. They won 31 of their next 40 games, losing two straight just once during that run. Three weeks after sweeping Philadelphia, they could confidently begin making World Series plans.

With the pennant long since clinched, the Americans won just one of six games in late September. Yearning to enter the first Fall Classic on a roll, they concluded the regular season with three straight victories over St. Louis, including a doubleheader sweep. The Pittsburgh Pirates awaited.

An annual clash to decide baseball supremacy was the brainchild of Pirates owner Barney Dreyfuss, but the seeds for such a showdown were planted by American League president Ban Johnson. He quickly established the AL as a threat to the senior circuit through player raids of the National League and lowering ticket prices to attract fans. The success of that strategy motivated NL officials to convoke peace negotiations that would allow both leagues to thrive. When it became apparent in September that his team and the Americans were destined to win pennants, Dreyfuss soon proposed to Boston owner Henry Killilea a best-of-nine battle between the two champions at season's end. The World Series was born.[9]

Dreyfuss might have regretted the offer by the time October 1 arrived. Superstar slugger Honus Wagner was trying to play through a leg injury. Pitcher Sam Leever's love for trapshooting led to a sore arm. And fellow starter Ed Doheny had grown mentally unbalanced. He bolted one game in the delusional fear that he was being followed by detectives and soon entered an insane asylum from which he would never emerge.[10]

The Huntington Avenue Grounds were packed for the first World Series game ever played. More than 16,000 fans besieged the park—nearly 5,000 above capacity. Some climbed the outfield wall to catch a glimpse of history. They stood in the outfield and infield as they awaited the first pitch. The luckiest bunch were the Royal Rooters. So enamored had the organization grown of the most loyal of loyalists that they allowed the bunch to sit in front of the stands behind home plate. As for wild pitches and passed balls fired in their direction? They didn't care nor, apparently, did anyone else.[11]

Perhaps such a sight unnerved Young and his teammates. Or perhaps the pressure of the moment wreaked havoc, but the first inning in World Series history was not one for the ages. Young allowed four runs, three unearned, thanks to three hits and two errors. The Americans never recovered in a 7–3 defeat.

It soon became apparent that Young would not be the pitching star of this event. That distinction belonged to Dinneen, who fired a three-hit shutout with 11 strikeouts in a 3–0 victory that sent the series to Pittsburgh even. The hitting hero of the game was equally clear. It was Dougherty, who slammed two homers, including an inside-the-park round-tripper leading off the first inning.

Young's next start was pushed back when he was forced to pitch seven innings of relief in a Game 3 defeat, then the Americans fell in Game 4 as well. He saved the series with a complete-game performance in Game 5, then Dinneen picked up where he left off. He shut out the Pirates for six innings in a 6–3 triumph in Game 6 to knot the series.

The pair proceeded to polish off Pittsburgh. Young overcame four errors to win, 7–3, sending the series back to Boston for a potential clincher and celebration. Two RBI singles by underappreciated second baseman Hobe Ferris provided more support than required for Dinneen, who hurled a four-hit shutout to give his team the first World Series championship. He fittingly fanned Wagner to end it.

Boston Herald sports journalist W. S. Barnes Jr. opened his story of the triumph with the following salute to the victors: "All hail to the Boston Americans, champion ball players of the world!"

Barnes later described a scene in the clubhouse that mixed politics and sports.

A pleasing incident was enacted in the Boston players' dressing room after the game yesterday when Senator M.J. Sullivan, himself an old ball player presented to Capt. James J. Collins on behalf of business manager Joseph Smart and the players of the team a costly gold watch and a handsome locket, in which was set a brilliant diamond. Senator Sullivan complimented Capt. Collins on his leadership and the magnificent work of his team, and said that the token from the players was in appreciation of his personal attitude toward them which was at all times kindly and considerate. The presentation was loudly applauded by the players. . . . Capt. Collins was completely taken aback and nearly broke down.[12]

Memories of that World Series title would eventually be clouded by those that followed before the trade of Ruth. But it was immortalized in 2004—the year the Curse was broken—by the Dropkick Murphys, a rock band formed in Quincy. The group remade a song called "Tessie," which honored the critical Game 5 victory over the Pirates and was adopted as an anthem by the Royal Rooters.

Boston baseball fans regret a lost opportunity in 1904 after their Americans won another pennant. Business wrangling between the two leagues resulted in a one-year hiatus for the World Series, the last time it would not be played until the 1994 strike. But the honor of winning the first World Series could never be taken away from the Americans or Boston baseball loyalists. And those that experienced it could thank the one-two pitching punch of Young and Dinneen for those fond memories.

CHAPTER TWO

Fenway and the *Monstah*

ONE CAN ARGUE THAT FENWAY PARK IS THE MOST LEGENDARY BASE-ball venue in America. That distinction and praise are generally reserved for Yankee Stadium, but those grounds are hallowed more for those that graced its field. There is a reason it is nicknamed The House That Ruth Built.

Yankee Stadium is fabled because Babe Ruth played in it. And DiMaggio. And Mantle. And because it was the site of 27 world championship teams. The greatness of Fenway Park is *Fenway Park*. It is inimitable for the Green Monster. Pesky Pole. The Triangle. The hand-operated scoreboard. All ballparks have personal touches that make them unique. But Fenway boasts a charm like no other. Each feature has become a legend within a legend. And that legend has continued to grow for more than a century.

The seeds were planted by owner John I. Taylor, whose father was General Charles Taylor, a newspaper magnate who had saved the *Boston Globe* from bankruptcy and bought the Americans in 1904 for about $150,000 to give his renegade son something to do. The offspring yearned to put his stamp on the team, changing its name to the Red Sox in 1907 and adding promotions such as Ladies Day, which allowed women to attend certain games free of charge and became a staple attraction for generations in ballparks across the country. Soon the young Taylor announced plans to abandon the Huntington Avenue Grounds for a new venue.[1]

The motivation was purely financial. The Taylors were by that time seeking to sell part of their ownership, but they did not own the current venue. They understood that such an arrangement would weaken sales opportunities, so they decided to have a new ballpark built on land they possessed. And that was a substantial but undeveloped tract in the Back Bay known as the "Fens." Folks called the surrounding area "Fenway," hence the future name of the new home of the Red Sox.

The park was only partially completed when it opened for an exhibition game between the Sox and Harvard University on April 9, 1912. A far more auspicious debut occurred against the Yankees before an estimated 24,000 fans eleven days later as the Sox won, 7–6, as spitball reliever Bucky O'Brien earned the victory in relief of Charlie "Sea Lion" Hall, whose deep voice inspired his nickname.[2]

Not that the trials and tribulations of the local baseball team were foremost in the hearts and minds of Bostonians that day. Or those in any other American city. For as the Red Sox were preparing for the grand opening of Fenway, survivors of the *Titanic* were mourning the dead and thankful they were making it back to New York with hearts still beating. Even the heartiest fans felt more driven to keep abreast of that news than how the new park was being received.

Fenway soon began to round into its unique form. It featured a single-deck grandstand of steel and concrete and 25-foot wooden fence in left built atop a 10-foot embankment later nicknamed "Duffy's Cliff" in honor of Red Sox left fielder Duffy Lewis. The original intent of building a high wall was to prevent fans on Lansdowne Street from getting a free peek of the action on the field.[3]

The park, built at a cost of $650,000, which barely exceeded the minimum one-year salary of a major-league *player* in 2018, seemed misaligned to those with conventional tastes. Walls jutted out in odd angles. The turf in left sloped strongly from the wall toward the infield. The fence at the deepest point in center was placed almost 550 feet from home plate, nearly double the distance from the right field fence, which was moved back 45 feet in the 1920s upon the construction of a new bleacher section.

Some believe the strange dimensions and barriers were inspired by fear that batted balls would strike structures in surrounding streets. But this is either untrue or such worry was certainly unfounded. After all, this was the Dead Ball Era. Babe Ruth had yet to don a Red Sox uniform. Nobody was slamming 400-foot home runs. The embankment in left made it easier for folks to see the game. The team allowed fans to sit behind the fielder, and the hill made it possible for those sitting in the back to watch the action. As the Dead Ball Era gave way to the Live Ball Era and more batted balls reached the left field fence, on-field tickets were sold only in the event of overflow crowds.[4]

The huge wooden wall in left was an advertiser's dream. The large, bold ads pitched everything from suits and hats to whiskey to biscuits. And excursions to Fenway proved quite convenient for patrons—more so than today—when a parking lot was built behind the outfield to take advantage of the explosion in the number of automobiles owned by the general public.

Despite the new venue and a team that had completed its rebound from a few lean years to win another World Series, attendance did not significantly increase. The Red Sox drew 94,000 more in 1912 than they had the previous season, which could have been more the result of a pennant-winning bunch than the move to Fenway. But aside from the distance from the center field stands that motivated a *Globe* cartoonist to show fans requiring telescopes to watch the game, the patrons seemed satisfied enough. After all, Boston did lead the American League in attendance that season.[5]

The most iconic feature in Fenway was known as nothing more than a tall wall for decades. But the wood structure remained a fire hazard. The threat turned into a blaze in May 1926 that began in the stands after the game had concluded. The cause remains unknown, but strong winds blew it throughout the section. The left field bleachers were destroyed. Another fire struck a few weeks later during a Red Sox–Yankees game.

Mother Nature picked up on July 19 where the fires left off. A powerful storm that ravaged New England that day triggered a tornado that slammed into the Fenway neighborhood. The ballpark did not take the brunt of the twister but did experience severe wind damage. The *Boston Globe* reported the following: "The wind leaped and wiped out two whole

This blaze nearly destroyed Fenway Park in 1912.
COURTESY OF THE BOSTON PUBLIC LIBRARY, LESLIE JONES COLLECTION

sections of seats, including 500 or 600 chairs. These were picked up and tossed bodily into the center of the grandstand, twisted and broken."[6]

The combination punch of fire and wind devastated Fenway. The burnt third-base bleachers went unrepaired. They remained in ruins until August, when they were finally hauled away. Rather than use the insurance money for restorations, Red Sox president Bob Quinn spent it on operating expenses. Fenway, a mere 14 years old, maintained the look of a dilapidated ballpark for the next eight seasons. It was an eyesore that aided only third basemen and catchers, who could race into foul territory once occupied by bleachers and snag foul balls.

If reconstruction seemed unlikely in the Roaring Twenties, one can imagine the impossibility of such a project when the Great Depression struck. But not everyone lost their shirts when the stock market crashed. Among those that maintained the wealth from a family fortune was Tom

Yawkey, who purchased the Red Sox for somewhere between $1 million and $1.2 million in 1933. Among his immediate goals was to transform the franchise from an on-field disaster to a contender and Fenway from a ghost town to a baseball mecca. The Sox emerged from their funk to play competitive baseball and the ballpark was revitalized.

Such success was not immediate. Fate took another nasty turn on January 5, 1934. That is when yet another fire, believed to have been started by a tipped-over heating stove inside the ballpark, devastated Fenway and spread beyond. The lone saving grace was that none of the more than 700 construction workers on the project was injured or killed—they were not in the park at the time. Neither was Yawkey, who was on a hunting excursion in South Carolina when he heard the news. Undaunted, he threw more money into saving Fenway. He spent more than a million bucks on the renovation. During a period of record unemployment, he hired enough workers to complete the job in time for the 1934 home opener.[7]

Among the upgrades was a new wall in left field that became the most iconic barrier in baseball. The Green Monster was born. The 37-foot behemoth constructed of concrete and tin, which would be covered in hard plastic in 1976, replaced the flammable wood structure. An added attraction was the hand-operated scoreboard that became a distinctive feature when all other ballparks adopted electronic displays. The thousands of Red Sox signatures, as well as those of other players passing through, strewn about the concrete base of the wall became another unique feature. Signing the wall became a veritable rite of passage for major leaguers.

The 12 feet added to the left field wall did not remove the threat of well-struck baseballs damaging Lansdowne Street businesses. The Green Monster, which remains the only barrier in baseball that regularly turns doubles or home runs into singles, loomed just 310 feet from home plate and the Dead Ball Era had been over for nearly 15 years. Fenway Park was the smallest venue in the sport. The result was a 23-foot-tall net placed above the wall in 1936 that prevented many baseballs from careening their way into danger mode. The problem of retrieving them "netted" another unique Fenway feature—the metal ladder that extends

The famous Fenway Park scoreboard and Green Monster.
WIKIMEDIA COMMONS

to the top of the wall in fair territory. Its presence sometimes wreaked havoc on outfielders as balls bouncing off it took strange routes that allowed batters to sprint for extra bases. One such doink off the ladder in 1963 famously sent a baseball far enough away to allow plodding Sox first baseman Dick Stuart to circle the bases for an inside-the-park home run.

Balls hit into the netting in batting practice and in games could only be retrieved by climbing the ladder. The irritating and time-consuming routine was made unnecessary in 2003, when 269 seats were placed above the Green Monster and the netting was removed. But the ladder remains as a reminder of the past and yet another quirk in the quirkiest ballpark in America.[8]

The final major renovation to the Green Monster had to wait until after World War II. The advertisements that many considered eyesores were removed in 1947 for a clean green look that fit Fenway far more scenically. Lights were also installed that year as the Red Sox proved late

The Pesky Pole has turned many long fly balls into home runs over the years.
WIKIMEDIA COMMONS

to the party. They were the third-last team in the majors to institute night baseball.

Another piece of history that was eventually transformed into a visual tribute occurred the season before on June 9, 1946. That is when Ted Williams launched a majestic 502-foot homer to right. It traveled to the right field bleachers—Section 42, Row 37, Seat 21 to be exact. The ball bounced off the straw hat worn by construction engineer Joseph A. Boucher and reportedly traveled a dozen rows higher. The blast is still considered the longest in Fenway Park history. Though the bleachers were benches at the time, the seat in the spot occupied by Boucher was painted red in 1984 to honor Williams and his prodigious blow.[9]

Among the other idiosyncrasies of Fenway is the Pesky Pole, which separates fair and foul territory down the right field line, a mere 302 feet from home plate (though some claim it to be shorter). The shortest home-run porch in baseball was named after slap-hitting shortstop Johnny

Pesky, who offered that he and ace pitcher Mel Parnell named it after the former won a game for the latter with a home run that curved around the pole into those cheap seats. That was indeed a rare occurrence—only six of Pesky's 17 career home runs were hit at Fenway. But the explanation has a huge hole. Pesky claimed the homer in question was hit in 1948. However, Pesky hit just one home run in a game pitched by Parnell at Fenway. That was on June 11, 1950. And that one came in the first inning of a game the Red Sox lost.

The more likely source of the nickname still involved Parnell. The two-time All-Star became a Red Sox broadcaster in 1965 and he often referred to the Pesky Pole. So popular proved that moniker that the Red Sox officially designated the right field foul pole as the Pesky Pole as part of the beloved infielder's birthday celebration in 2006.[10]

Indeed, the Pesky Pole is just one reason that Fenway is a major attraction unto itself. That cannot be claimed about many ballparks in America. Perhaps, in his inimitable way, legendary Sox lefty Bill "Spaceman" Lee expressed it best when he said, "Fenway Park is a shrine. People go there to worship."[11]

Chapter Three

The Annual Champs

What was the first dynasty in baseball history? One might claim it to be the Chicago White Stockings, which won six National League pennants from 1876 to 1886. Or the Boston Beaneaters, which earned five NL crowns a decade later. How about the New York Giants? They snagged five National League championships in the early 1900s. But they took only one World Series in the process.

Picky evaluators who save such proclamations for teams that distinguished themselves in the regular season and beyond claim the first dynasty to have been earned by the Boston Red Sox from 1912 to 1918. The initial occupiers of Fenway and teammates of Babe Ruth won four World Series titles during that seven-year period. And two of those ultimate triumphs (1915 and 1916) were gained despite what can be claimed in hindsight as the epic managerial blunder of utilizing the Sultan of Swat only on the mound. The level of such a mistake cannot be compared to that of sending The Babe packing to the Big Apple, which, it can be argued, killed the dynasty. But one wonders given that Ruth had emerged as the most prodigious masher in the Dead Ball Era just how dominant the Sox would have been had manager Bill Carrigan found a way to stick him in the everyday lineup.

Ruth was a 17-year-old playing for the St. Mary's Industrial School for Boys and still two years from the first game of his short-lived minor-league career when the Red Sox embarked on their dominant 1912 season. Fans streamed into spanking-new Fenway Park to watch the premier hitting team in the league, led by the outfield tandem of future Hall

The proud 1915 American League champion Red Sox.
WIKIMEDIA COMMONS

of Famers Harry Hooper and Tris Speaker, who was named AL Most Valuable Player. The trio of Hooper, Speaker, and Duffy Lewis combined for 319 runs scored. Meanwhile, ace "Smoky" Joe Wood compiled a record of 34-5, which remains the second-best winning percentage of any 30-game-winning right-hander in baseball history. Wood and fellow 20-game winners Buck O'Brien and Hugh Bedient were among four starters that finished with WHIPs (walks and hits to innings pitched) under 1.2.

The 1912 Sox climbed atop the standings on June 15 and remained there the rest of the year. But the lopsided nature of the race did not preclude moments of drama. The peak of suspense occurred in a September 6 showdown between Wood and already legendary Washington right-hander Walter Johnson, who would win 33 games that year and lead the league with a 1.39 ERA. Wood had won 13 consecutive decisions to threaten Johnson's American League record of 16. An estimated 29,000 fans packed Fenway that Friday afternoon to watch the two fireballers match their talents at the peak of their careers. *Boston Globe* sportswriter Melville Webb wrote the following to describe the scene:

The crowds packed the stands and the bleachers and trooped all over the outfield inside the stand and bleacher boundaries. In the grandstand the broad promenade was packed solid ten rows deep with fans on tiptoes to see what was going on. The playing field was surrounded completely by a triple, even quadruple, rank of humanity, at least 3,000 assembling on the banking in left field, and the mass of enthusiasts around in front of the huge concrete stand. . . . So thickly were the spectators massed, and so impossible was it for the squadron of police to keep them back, that the players' pits were abandoned, the contestants bringing their war clubs out almost to the baselines.[1]

Those fans did not leave the ballpark disappointed. Wood hurled a six-inning shutout with nine strikeouts in a taut 1–0 triumph made possible when Lewis doubled in Speaker in the sixth inning. The victory completed a 10-game winning streak that removed all doubt as to the American League champion. So memorable proved that Wood-Johnson battle that Hooper recalled it with relish years later. And in a current era in which Major League Baseball and younger fans become sickened at the thought of a pitcher's battle, the recollections of Hooper take on added relevance. "That was probably the most exciting game I ever played in or saw," Hooper said. And when asked to compare the fastest of the fast, Hooper added, "Listen, my friend, there's no man alive can throw harder than Smoky Joe Wood."[2]

Red Sox manager Jake Stahl rode his flame-throwing ace in the World Series against ace counterpart Christy Mathewson and the Giants. But what was feared to be interference from team owner James McAleer threatened to cost Boston the championship. Wood was scheduled to pitch what could have been a clinching Game 6 (Game 2 ended in a tie, which lengthened the series), but it was believed that McAleer yearned for another home date with Wood on the mound, ensuring a Fenway sellout. The Red Sox players anticipated that Wood would pitch but learned differently after an argument between Stahl and McAleer during the train trip to New York. O'Brien started instead and got knocked out after one inning in a 5–2 defeat.

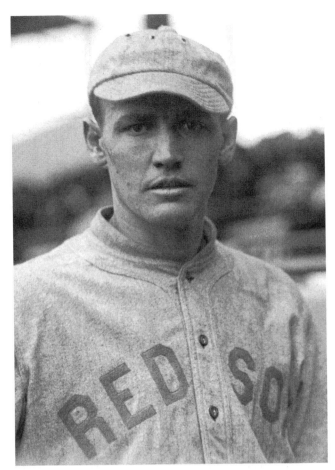

Smoky Joe Wood won 57 games combined in 1911 and 1912 for the Red Sox.
WIKIMEDIA COMMONS

The maneuver that failed all but McAleer's bottom line could have proven disastrous. He compounded fears of impending doom when he booted the Royal Rooters from their customary seats, which were sold to other fans, causing a riot that required the intervention of mounted police. Making matters worse, Wood's arm tightened before facing the Giants in Game 7 and he too was thrashed in the first inning. And even McAleer did not benefit much when a coin flip determined that the deciding Game 8 would be played at Fenway. The fans stayed away in droves to protest the treatment of the Royal Rooters—only 17,000 showed up to see Bedient pitch Mathewson to a draw. New York took a 2–1 lead in a thrilling 10th inning, but Giants center fielder Fred Snodgrass's muff of an easy flyball set an unlikely comeback in motion. An RBI single by Speaker and sacrifice fly by Larry Gardner gave the victory to Wood, who had pitched the last three innings, and the World Series triumph to the Red Sox.

Sadly, it was Wood's last hurrah at age 25. He slipped on some wet grass the following spring training and broke his right thumb. That threw off his pitching motion and he developed shoulder soreness. It has also been speculated that throwing 344 innings in 1912 played a role in Wood's demise. Though he performed well from 1913 to 1915, even winning an ERA title in the last of those years, he was used only sporadically. Wood maxed out at 157 innings in 1915, briefly tried to resuscitate his career as an outfielder, and was out of baseball at the age of 30.

The conundrum of replacing the production of Wood proved secondary to the loss of offense in 1913 and 1914. The emergence of Dutch Leonard and rise of Ray Collins offset the fall of Wood and collapse of O'Brien, who proved to be a one-year wonder. The Red Sox scored 117 fewer runs in 1913 than they had the previous season. They fell 12 games out of first place by the end of May, costing Stahl his managerial job in favor of catcher Bill Carrigan. The Sox fared better in 1914, but never spent a day in first place as they chased the Philadelphia Athletics in vain and spoiled an epic season from the lefty Leonard, whose 0.96 ERA remains the best in modern baseball history.

Another southpaw made his debut in 1914 and emerged as one of the premier pitchers in the sport over the next two seasons. His name was George Herman Ruth. But the Sox starting staff boasted so much talent and depth in 1915 that his 2.44 ERA that year was the *worst* among the quintet. Despite a lineup that managed a mere 14 home runs (Ruth led the team with four in just 92 at-bats) and in which once again its only significant producers were outfielders Speaker, Hooper, and Lewis, the Red Sox roared to another pennant. They fell six games behind in late

June, but blitzes of 11-1 and 10-1 in July pushed them into the lead. The Sox won 18 of 21 in August and later added two seven-game winning streaks, but they couldn't tame the Tigers, who hung around nearly all season. Boston finally beat Detroit three times in a four-game series that drew 105,000 fans to Fenway in late September to all but put the pennant away, though it was not clinched until they beat the host Yankees in the first game of a doubleheader on October 6.

The Sox decided to abandon Fenway for the greater-capacity Braves Field for their World Series games (which they did as well in 1916). So balanced was the Boston staff that Ruth and Wood were banished to the bullpen. Ernie Shore, Rube Foster, and Leonard made quick work of Philadelphia, sweeping the Athletics after a Game 1 defeat. Nary a Sox reliever graced the mound as the trio hurled five consecutive complete games, compiling a 1.84 ERA and an unearthly 0.84 WHIP. Most impressive was the pressure they overcame given that the world championship hung in the balance and that their bat-wielding teammates offered little support.

Ruth emerged as the unquestioned ace of a 1916 rotation that lost Wood, who remained at his Pennsylvania home ostensibly to treat his ailing arm. The Babe overcame control problems to compile a 23-12 record and 1.75 ERA. The emergence of right-hander Carl Mays, who later gained the dubious distinction as the overaggressive sidearmer whose fastball killed Indians infielder Ray Chapman, also helped offset the absence of Wood. The more significant loss was that of Speaker, who was swapped to Cleveland for pitcher Sad Sam Jones, who managed two strong seasons with the Sox, and nondescript third baseman Fred Thomas.

The departures of Wood and Speaker, who were best friends, are steeped in controversy. It has been claimed that both yearned to leave for political reasons. The Texan Speaker was a member of the Ku Klux Klan at its height of popularity that followed the release of the film *Birth of a Nation*. The contention is that neither Speaker nor Wood got along with their Catholic teammates—particularly Ruth, Lewis, and Hooper.[3]

If such assertions were true and the exoduses of Speaker and Wood positively affected the Sox, it was not evident on the field early in the year. They took what was now becoming a familiar path of playing fol-

Sidearmer Carl Mays emerged as a Sox standout in the late 1910s.
WIKIMEDIA COMMONS

low-the-leader into midseason before surging. They dropped six games off the pace in June and managed to creep only to five games over .500 in early July before hitting their stride. They swept four from contending Chicago to embark on a 17-6 run, took three of four from the same Sox in August to sneak into first place, then went 12-2 down the stretch to clinch the pennant.

Boston was again peaking at the right time as a World Series showdown against Brooklyn approached. This time Ruth would take a back seat to none of his fellow starters. He crafted the best performance of the event, a complete-game, 14-inning masterpiece in which he allowed just one run in a 2–1 victory. Shore polished off the Robins by going nine and giving up just one unearned tally in a 4–1 victory. The Red Sox were again world champions.

The lack of offensive punch finally took a major toll in 1917. Only Lewis batted above .265 among the starters as fans cried in vain for Ruth to be used more as an outfielder. The Sox staff compiled a 2.20 ERA, the lowest during their seven-year dynasty that ended a year later. But Boston finished fourth in the American League in runs scored, a flaw that proved fatal in their vain chase of the White Sox, who won 18 of 19 in late August and early September to put the pennant away.

The question of how best to utilize Ruth fell on the shoulders in 1918 of new manager Ed Barrow, who had been named to the post by new owner Harry Frazee. Barrow knew that he had already lost Lewis, his best hitter, who had enlisted to fight in World War I. He knew that Ruth wanted to play every day and boasted the potential to lead the American League in home runs. But he also knew that Leonard had retired to take a job in a shipyard, leaving a hole in the rotation. Barrow decided he wanted Ruth to pitch full-time.

That was his role early in the 1918 season—and Ruth rebelled. He played the field only sporadically until early June but yearned desperately to land a lineup spot when not on the mound. He even expressed disdain for pitchers who could not help themselves from the batter's box. "The pitcher who can't get in there in the pinch and win his own game with a healthy wallop isn't more than half earning his salary to my way of thinking," he said. "I am a pitcher myself and I like to pitch. But if there is one thing that appeals to me more than winning a close game from a tough rival, it's knocking out a good, clean three-bagger with men on base."[4]

That is exactly what he did to convince Barrow to utilize him daily. Ruth tripled in two runs to tie a game, leading to more play in the outfield and first base. He finished the regular season, which was cut short as the war came to a head on September 2, with 11 home runs to tie for the American League lead in just 317 at-bats. But it was his pitching down the stretch and in the World Series that wowed baseball. Ruth won nine of his last 11 decisions, lowering his ERA from 2.83 to 2.21 in the process. He surrendered two or fewer runs in nine of his final 10 starts to help the Sox stave off the competition and win their fourth pennant in seven years. Ruth then blanked the Cubs in the opener (the first time "The Star-Spangled Banner" was played at a sporting event) and pitched seven consecutive scoreless innings in a Game 4 victory to run his World Series scoreless streak to 29⅔ innings, a major-league record that remained until 1961. The Red Sox scored just 10 runs in the six-game series but held Chicago to nine to win their fourth Series crown in as many attempts since 1912.

That Ruth was the most prolific slugger of his era is a given. But those fortunate enough to have seen him before he became exclusively a position player rave about his talent on the mound. In the landmark Ken Burns documentary detailing the history of the sport, journalist and author Dan Okrent stated that Ruth was "the best left-handed pitcher of the 1910s without question, in the American League."[5]

The best left-hander of the 1910s was not long for the mound, though the complete abdication would have to wait until he donned a Yankees uniform. Barrow finally gave into pressure and utilized Ruth as a regular outfielder in 1919, though the manager apparently found it unrealistic to continue pitching him every fourth day. The result was that Ruth began revolutionizing the sport in earnest that year, blasting 29 home runs to set an MLB record he would nearly double in 1920. But not only had his number of starts been cut from 41 to 20 over two seasons, but he pitched less effectively. Ruth's WHIP soared from 1.046 in 1918 to a terrible 1.545 in 1919. He would make just five more starts the rest of his career.

Not that Barrow has been praised historically for keen foresight for transforming Ruth into an everyday player. Hooper later claimed to have formed a strategic alliance along with Red Sox shortstop Everett Scott and fading infielder Heinie Wagner to steer Barrow in the right direction. Hooper believed that Barrow made the transition Ruth preferred only through pressure. "He did it reluctantly and against his convictions," Hooper said. "Ruth came to be in the spring of 1919. He said he wanted to play the outfield. He thought he'd be more valuable to the club there than as a pitcher.... Barrow's argument was reasonable. He protested he'd be crazy to take the best young left-hander in the league and make an outfielder out of him. He said he'd be laughed to scorn by the fans if the

Early Sox standouts (left to right) Harry Hooper, Tris Speaker, and Duffy Lewis at an old-timers event in 1939.
COURTESY OF THE BOSTON PUBLIC LIBRARY, LESLIE JONES COLLECTION

experiment failed. . . . And I can recall Ed's words when he agreed. 'All right, I'll put Ruth out there, but mark my words, after the first slump he gets into, he'll come back on his knees begging to pitch again.'"[6]

That didn't happen, even after Ruth's batting average sunk to .180 in late May. A 14-game hitting streak in June pushed his average to .326 and he remained over .300 the rest of the season. But though Ruth didn't slump, his team did. They finished under .500 for the first time since 1908. Meanwhile, an idea that would come to fruition and cause arguably more heartache to a fan base than any in baseball history was fomenting in the mind of owner Harry Frazee. The long nightmare for Red Sox fans was about to begin.

CHAPTER FOUR

Creating the Curse

THE SEEDS FOR THE MOST NOTORIOUS TRADE IN BASEBALL HISTORY were not planted after Boston had concluded a disappointing 1919 season. Those seeds of discontent in the heart and mind of owner Harry Frazee were planted during the last World Series his team would win until 75 years after his death.

Frazee had lost money in 1918. Even the Fall Classic proved a financial failure. Only 60,000 fans trekked to Fenway over the last three games, including a mere 15,000 for the title clincher. Frazee was enjoying no more success in theater production. His plays were flopping. So he began trading away premier players for money—with the wealthy Yankees as the chief beneficiary. The Sox swapped top pitchers Dutch Leonard and Ernie Shore, as well as veteran left fielder Duffy Lewis to the soon-to-be Bronx Bombers for four nondescript players and $15,000.

Seven months later Carl Mays, another top hurler, made it easier for Frazee. The foul-tempered right-hander bolted a ballgame in July after catcher Wally Schang inadvertently nailed him in the head rather than nailing a baserunner trying to steal second. Mays vowed never to pitch for Boston again—and he got his wish when Frazee sold him to the Yankees for $40,000. American League president Ban Johnson was forced to relent to the deal when the Yankees, Red Sox, and White Sox threatened to bolt to the National League.[1]

The novelty of Fenway had certainly worn off for the fans in 1919, when postwar interest skyrocketed throughout baseball. More folks frequented Fenway as well, but the jump was far less significant as the Red

Sox owner and villain Harry Frazee, who sent Babe Ruth packing to the Yankees.
WIKIMEDIA COMMONS

Sox placed fifth among eight teams in American League attendance. Frazee still owed previous team owner Joseph Lannin money on the purchase of the ballpark. That too contributed to his financial miseries.

The highly respected Society for American Baseball Research claims that Frazee's profits from his theater business fell from $68,192 to around $5,000 in 1918 and 1919. His tax return in 1920 showed a loss of $42,534. Frazee yearned desperately to return his production business into the black. Despite his struggles he purchased the Harris Theater in New York through a $310,000 mortgage to finance the play *No, No, Nanette*.[2]

Many baseball historians offer that the desire to deal Ruth extended beyond financial considerations. Author and sportswriter Glenn Stout claimed in his book *The Selling of the Babe* that the future Sultan of Swat proved far less than an ideal teammate or human being during his days in Boston. Stout asserted that Ruth had to be removed from his Game 4 performance in the 1918 World Series due to a swollen finger that resulted from a punch he landed on a steel wall, window, or face of an unfortunate recipient during the train trip from Chicago to Boston. Stout further contended that Ruth's penchant for womanizing and gambling (which resulted in him losing a year's salary in a few weeks and forced the team to pay him on a per diem basis) alienated and frustrated teammates and others in the organization. Though Ruth proved himself gregarious, his devil-may-care attitude and indiscretions negatively affected his relationships. Wrote Stout:

> *Finding Ruth after a bender—usually sleeping if off somewhere, often in the back alley behind a brothel, his pockets turned inside out— became something of a pastime for his teammates. Stories of Ruth's nighttime escapades were well known among Boston working men . . . and some of their wives . . . Ruth loved to gamble but didn't really seem to get the concept that he was supposed to win.*[3]

Stout refuted the widely believed notion that Frazee sold Ruth to fund *No, No, Nanette*, offering instead that factors such as competition for the entertainment dollar with the crosstown Braves and the banning in Boston of Sunday home games proved more financially problematic.

So did Ruth's salary demand. Ruth understood his growing value after pounding 29 home runs and leading the league in RBIs in 1919. He wanted to escape his three-year contract and sign a new one for 1920 for $20,000. Frazee felt cornered by a confluence of circumstances seemingly beyond his control. He needed money and he needed it fast. He began sending overtures about dealing Ruth. That willingness became apparent when he stated that his only untradeable commodity was Hooper. Yankees owners Jacob Ruppert and T. J. Houston, whose acquisitions of Lewis and Mays had helped their team emerge as a contender for the first time since 1910, were quite happy to listen. They understood the competitive advantages and draw Ruth could provide—his sins could be hidden far better in New York than in conservative and Catholic-dominated Boston. Nobody, however, could have imagined that Ruth would revolutionize the sport and become a larger-than-life superstar, least of all Frazee.

Negotiations moved quickly. Ruth was traded to the Yankees on December 26, 1919 as quite the holiday kick-in-the-teeth for Red Sox fans. Frazee received $25,000 and three promissory notes for the same amount, as well as a $300,000 loan. He had promised Barrow ballplayers in return, but the manager replied that he preferred a straight cash deal to the embarrassment of putting an inferior talent in a Red Sox uniform, leaving a perception to the fans that the trade piece or pieces constituted Ruth's replacement.

Frazee offered the public a different explanation, stating that he would have preferred to get players back, but that the slugger had become so valuable that it would have proven impossible for the Yankees to make

The immortal Babe Ruth in 1918 before he was shipped to New York.
WIKIMEDIA COMMONS

an even swap without ruining their team. He also claimed that he would take the money received and pour it back into the franchise. After all, Boston had finished sixth in the American League with Ruth. Trading for premier ballplayers and paying them with Yankee money indeed seemed viable. But it never happened. The Red Sox were about to fall into the baseball abyss.

Not that the fan base was turning cartwheels upon learning of his departure. Ruth had emerged as a Beantown icon. Some joker, noting a poster for Frazee's play titled *My Lady Friends*, snorted, "They're the only friends that SOB has." Meanwhile, a cartoon appeared in the Boston papers the next day showing historic Faneuil Hall and the Boston Public Library with For Sale signs. The insinuation was obvious. If Ruth could be sold, so could the most famous landmarks in town.[4]

The *Globe* notoriously and with lack of foresight applauded the move, claiming that if the Red Sox could continue to win championships following the departures of Cy Young and Tris Speaker, the loss of Ruth would not preclude them from snagging more crowns. The article suggested that a weak knee made Ruth susceptible to injury and that the money Frazee received could purchase several players that could help the team regain its status as a pennant contender. The *Globe* also cautioned that the swap might not even be consummated. The newspaper quoted a telegram from Ruth to business manager Johnny Igoe in which he stated he would not play anywhere but Boston, where he had invested heavily in a cigar business that required his frequent presence. But the article also stated that New York manager Miller Huggins claimed he had already signed Ruth.[5] And veteran *Globe* beat writer Dan Shaughnessy wrote decades later that Ruth had embraced the potential deal from the moment he first learned of it two weeks earlier.[6]

Indeed, the Yankees' offer to Ruth assuaged any objections. He received an immediate raise and his earlier request of the Red Sox for a $20,000 contract was met after the 1920 season (it would reach $52,000 by 1922). But Frazee blasted the budding superstar on the way out, adding fuel to the fire for historians who believed Ruth was dispatched more for personal reasons than for financial considerations. "It would be impossible to start next season with Ruth and have a smooth-working machine," he said. "Ruth has become simply impossible and the Boston club could no longer put up with his eccentricities. I think the Yankees are taking a gamble. While Ruth is undoubtedly the greatest hitter the game has ever seen, he is likewise one of the most selfish and inconsiderate men ever to put on a baseball uniform."[7]

Such did not become the legacy of Babe Ruth. He grew into a larger-than-life figure who did more to popularize and revolutionize baseball than any player in history. He gained a reputation as a fun-loving, big-hearted slugger who embraced opportunities to work with kids. He became a symbol of the carefree Roaring Twenties. And he transformed the Yankees into a powerhouse in American sport. Meanwhile, the Red Sox sank to the depths, descending rapidly from perennial champions into the worst darn team in baseball. The fall of the Red Sox that coincided with the rise of the Yankees remains perhaps the most intriguing plot twist in the history of the sport. But it was certainly no coincidence. It will forever be traced back to the swap of the Sultan of Swat.

CHAPTER FIVE

The Morass

OPENING DAY 1923. DISBANDED FIVE YEARS EARLIER, THE ROYAL Rooters had become a distant memory. Prohibition had doomed the iconic McGreevey's Third Base Saloon. And the eventual world champion Yankees could now be considered Red Sox South. Eleven players on their roster had once called Fenway Park home.

The death of a dynasty came quickly following the sale of Babe Ruth to New York. Not that the Sox immediately slipped into misery and despair—they finished with virtually the same winning percentage in 1920 and 1921 as they had in 1919. They even opened their first season without Ruth on a 21-9 run that placed them atop the American League. But they fell hopelessly behind by early June in both seasons as formerly faithful fans lost interest. The Red Sox finished last in attendance in 1921. And while Ruth was busy slugging 113 total home runs in those two years, Boston ranked last in launching longballs both seasons with a meager 39 *combined*.

While The Great Bambino single-handedly destroyed the Dead Ball Era by whacking baseballs over fences at a pace unthinkable just a few years earlier, his spot in left field at Fenway had been taken by the eminently forgettable "Leaping Mike" Menosky, who managed decent numbers, but managed a mere nine home runs in four years with Boston.

And if the woebegone Red Sox fans thought their team had hit rock bottom, they had another thing coming. The 1921 model was a Rolls Royce compared to the 1922 bunch. Boston finished last that year for the first time since 1906. Despite nearly tripling their home-run total from

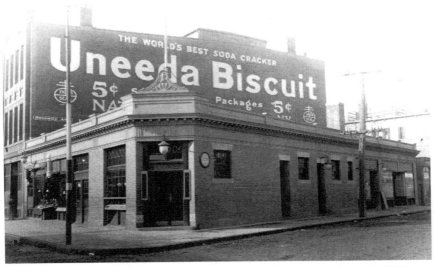

The legendary Third Base Saloon in the Roxbury Crossing neighborhood in 1916.
BOSTON PUBLIC LIBRARY.

the previous season they ranked last in runs scored. And a pitching staff that a mere four years earlier boasted the likes of Ruth, Mays, Leonard, and Bullet Joe Bush (who had *also* been traded to the Yankees and posted a 26-7 record that season) ranked among the worst in baseball.

The unraveling of the Red Sox during the early 1920s was aided by none other than former manager Ed Barrow, who was encouraged by Frazee to follow Ruth to New York and take a job in the Yankee front office. Barrow continued to formulate deals that resulted in the Red Sox languishing at or near the bottom of the standings and New York launching the greatest dynasty in the history of American sport. Included among those traded from the Red Sox to the Yankees were future Hall of Fame pitchers Waite Hoyt and Herb Pennock. The latter was swapped for $50,000.

"All Frazee wanted was the money," said standout outfielder Harry Hooper, who was sent to the White Sox before the 1921 season. "He was

"Nuf Ced" Ned McGreevy started the Royal Rooters in the early 1900s.

short on cash and he sold the whole team down the river to keep his dirty nose above water. What a way to end a wonderful ballclub! I got sick to my stomach at the whole business. . . . I was glad to get away from that graveyard."[1]

What was once a proud franchise had lost its way. Heck, they were the Red Sox only in name in 1922—they didn't even wear red socks that year. What was assumed to be a welcome development on July 11, 1923, when Frazee sold the team to a group of midwesterners headed by St. Louis Browns general manager Bob Quinn, resulted in disaster as the syndicate proved itself economically unable to fulfill its obligations. The *Sporting News*, which had been called the baseball bible, even suggested that the date that Frazee unloaded the Red Sox should be deemed a local holiday. But soon the Sox descended from poor to pathetic.[2]

The financial collapse that exacerbated the competitive one was born from bad luck rather than bad intent. The ownership group depended greatly upon Indiana glass manufacturer Palmer Winslow to make the investment a success. But Winslow died without providing money for his partners. Rather than sell the team, Quinn decided to keep it. He was left with a terrible club and no cash to improve it. It has even been suggested that he started the fire at Fenway in May 1926 to collect badly needed insurance money.[3]

The Red Sox of the late 1920s and early 1930s experienced one of the worst stretches in major-league history. They lost at least 90 games every year from 1925 to 1932 when they sported records of 47-105, 46-107, 51-103, 57-96, 58-96, 52-102, 62-90, and 43-111. They finished last every year but 1931—and any optimism gained from escaping the cellar was dashed when they stumbled to their worst mark in franchise history in 1932. Their rosters remained painfully young and untalented throughout. When an occasional gem arrived such as right-hander Red Ruffing, he was sold by Quinn. Naturally, Ruffing was sent to the Yankees, where he blossomed into one of the premier pitchers during their first dynasty and earned a spot in the Hall of Fame.

Not that anyone in Boston seemed to care by that time. The Red Sox ranked near the bottom of the American League in attendance annually. Their lone draw, ironically and pathetically, were the Yankees. Fans flocked to watch Ruth crank homers over the wall in left. In 1927, when Ruth shattered his home single-season home-run record with 60 and no Boston player hit more than six, the Red Sox averaged fewer than 4,000 fans per home game. But Ruth and his Bronx Bombers attracted at least seven crowds of 15,000 or more, including a sellout for an early September doubleheader. Ruth managed just one hit that afternoon but made up for it the next day with two home runs as Pennock rubbed salt in the wound by hurling a complete-game victory.

The Dead Ball Era was long over, but the Red Sox failed to get the message. They ranked among the bottom three in the American League in home runs every year from 1923 to 1935. The team would often feature just one or two strong hitters in the lineup. Included was right fielder Earl Webb, who finally emerged in his early 30s in 1931 to smash 67 doubles, an American League record that still stood in 2018. Webb even hit 14 homers and drove in 103 runs that year to finish sixth in the Most Valuable Player balloting.

Boston players of that era felt sorry for each other. Rather than mourn the loss of a teammate via trade, they celebrated his good fortune. "You couldn't do anything for a ballclub like that, though there was no use complaining because they were, after all, all your friends," explained Red Sox pitcher Milt Gaston, who himself was dealt to the White Sox after the 1931 season. "So you just took it with a grain of salt. When Ruffing got traded to the Yankees, we were glad for him. Any time a guy left the club, we were glad for him, because he couldn't have gone to a worse club."[4]

Stories abound throughout baseball history about flakes and misfits drifting through struggling organizations, and the Red Sox of this unfortunate era were no exception. Among their most notable was right-handed pitcher Big Ed Morris, who had been bouncing around the minors for six years since his cup of coffee with the Cubs in 1922. Only the Sox were desperate enough to give him a chance. They signed him for $10,000 and invited him to spring training in 1928. Though Morris impressed the Red Sox brass with his raw stuff, opposing batters were not fooled and slammed line drives all around the park. He performed well enough in Florida to be ticketed for Boston. There was just one hitch. He was in jail as the regular season was set to start. Morris hated policemen as much as he liked to drink. *Boston Record* beat writer Joe Cashman reported that Morris had a penchant for pulling the buttons off cop coats, resulting in a few slams over the head with a nightstick. Red Sox manager Bill Carrigan suggested that Morris remain in the slammer until May, but the skipper was so desperate for pitching he had tabbed the journeyman to be second in his rotation. He bailed out Morris, who made his way to Boston.[5]

Morris either stayed off the sauce or handled it well enough to positively contribute that season. He easily led the team with 19 wins and five saves while compiling a respectable 3.53 ERA. His 1.30 WHIP was the best among an albeit ragtag group of starters. As one might expect, however, Morris began slip-sliding away, raising his ERA nearly one point in 1929. Arm problems that some have claimed stemmed from a fight with Detroit police signaled the beginning of the end of his viability as a major-league pitcher. But his last start in 1931 provided some encouragement. He pitched a complete game victory over the St. Louis Browns.

The Alabaman had given himself and the locals from the town of Flomaton hope. His buddies planned a fish fry as part of a farewell bash at a cabin along the Conecuh River just before spring training in 1932. The details that followed remain clouded in mystery, but what is known is that Morris knocked down attendee Joe White, who accused the pitcher of flirting with his wife even though the former was married with two kids. An enraged White responded by taking out a knife and stabbing Morris near the heart.

What happened next has been claimed in two wildly different stories. Cashman offered that Morris jumped in the river and died of pneumonia rather than the stabbing. But other reports state he drove himself to the hospital and survived for a few days before succumbing to his wounds. Yet another version of the incident asserts that it was a man named Joe Nolan with whom Morris argued and White was simply acting as peacemaker. That story contends that Morris without provocation began punching and kicking White, who at that point stabbed his assailant.[6]

Either way, Morris died before he could experience a noteworthy event in Red Sox history. The city of Boston had finally allowed Sunday baseball in 1929, but games could not be played at Fenway due to its proximity to a church. They were forced to play their Sunday home games a mile away at Braves Field. Nobody had thought to ask the minister of the church whether he had any moral or practical objections to the Sox playing Sunday games at Fenway, which sat a mere 100 yards away. The minister said no. After all, the games were scheduled after services had concluded. So the Red Sox finally hosted a Sunday game on July 3. Their disturbingly horrible record of 14-56 limited the crowd to an estimated 9,000 despite the presence of the Yankees, whose novelty as an opponent had apparently worn off. And, as one might have guessed, Babe and the boys battered Boston, 13–2.[7]

The Sox had hit rock bottom. It would take new ownership to save them from drowning.

CHAPTER SIX

The Yawkey Way

THE MOST IMPORTANT FIGURE IN RED SOX HISTORY WAS NOT CY YOUNG or Ted Williams or Carl Yastrzemski or David Ortiz. It was not Joe Cronin or Terry Francona. The most important figure in Red Sox history never wore a Red Sox uniform. It was Tom Yawkey. The owner of 41 years not only lifted the franchise from the economic and competitive depths to which it had sunk in the 1920s and early 1930s but maintained its viability on the field throughout his tenure. He trusted those he hired and avoided the meddlesome tactics of more publicity-driven baseball owners such as George Steinbrenner. And he ensured family ownership for 26 years after his death in 1976.

Thomas Yawkey Austin was born into wealth in 1903. His namesake father, whom he never got to know, married into a Yawkey family that had struck it rich in the timber and mining industries of the Midwest. His dad purchased an island of timber in Ontario, Canada, and settled into the family's estate in Detroit. But tragedy struck when the infant Yawkey was a mere seven months old. His father died, motivating his mother to move the family into the home of her brother William Yawkey. After Tom's mother died in 1918, Tom's Uncle Bill Adopted him, and he took Yawkey as his last name.

Bill Yawkey established a lifestyle for the young boy. The former was not the industrious type who toiled to increase his fortune. Rather, he enjoyed hunting, drinking, gambling on the horses, and spending time with ballplayers as a co-owner of the Tigers. The elder Yawkey preferred to enjoy his wealth and proved a positive influence. He showed his son the value of treating his ballplayers well, a lesson the boy would embrace for a lifetime. Under the Yawkey ownership, the Tigers soared from the depths to the heights, winning three consecutive pennants. He not only spent money on player salaries but gave it to them frivolously for small accomplishments. He hung out with his players at bars and paid for the tab. He instilled in Tom a love for the sport and introduced him to stars such as Ty Cobb and Eddie Collins. Tom attended the prestigious Irving School, where Collins had starred a generation earlier, and emerged as a fine ballplayer in his own right.

The death of his mother and adopted father six months apart impacted Tom beyond his grief. He was left with a fortune estimated between $7 million and $20 million. That money was destined to remain in the hands of conservators until the 16-year-old Yawkey reached 30. He lived the life of luxury in the meantime, marrying a former beauty queen and accumulating wealth through little work of his own. There was not much to think about—he already knew what he wanted to do with his life. He yearned to own a baseball team like his dad did. He even instructed Collins, who by then had become a coach for the Philadelphia Athletics, to keep his ear to the ground and let him know if a major-league team came up for sale. After all, he would be in control of that fortune in 1933.

Enter the Boston Red Sox. No team in baseball was in greater need for fresh leadership and big bucks. They were coming off a 111-loss season, the worst in franchise history. Fewer than 3,000 fans per game trickled into Fenway in 1932. The roster was devoid of talent. And owner Robert Quinn wanted out. While attending the World Series, he ran into Collins, who recalled the conversation with Yawkey. About five months later, Yawkey bought the Red Sox and Fenway Park for the then-hefty price of $1.25 million. And though Collins felt a sense of loyalty to Athletics manager Connie Mack, who had promised to turn the club over to him, he accepted the job offered by Yawkey as the first general manager in Sox history.[1]

Yawkey explained his passion for baseball and hinted at his ownership philosophy during an interview with local sportswriter Dan Daniel in 1937, just four years after taking charge. It reflected his upbringing and relationship with his departed father. "Some men like to spend their dough on fast horses and other things that go fast," he said. "Some men like to go in for polo, for example, and spend thousands of dollars on ponies. Some go nuts for paintings and give half a million for a hunk of canvas in a fancy frame. But my passion is baseball. My idea of heaven is a pennant winner. Boston would go nuts over a winner, and maybe someday we'll get all the dough back. But in the meantime, don't let anybody tell you Tom Yawkey is a sucker."[2]

Yawkey had two risky but potentially rewarding choices on how to spend his money upon taking over the Sox. He could sign the most promising young talent from the many independent minor leagues that peppered the baseball landscape. Or he could acquire proven, but sometimes aging, major-league talent. He chose the latter course. The benefits proved immediate. He quickly sent players or cash (in the height of the Great Depression) for veterans, including future Hall of Fame catcher Rick Ferrell and hard-hitting second baseman Johnny Hodapp. Under the ownership of Yawkey and keen strategizing of Collins, the 1933 Red Sox raised their win total by 20 as the most improved team in Major League Baseball. They even flirted with .500 by the end of July after a 29-17 run.

The rise of the Red Sox began in earnest the following year after Yawkey purchased standout third baseman Billy Weber and traded for premier pitchers Wes Ferrell and Lefty Grove, whose miserable 1934 was followed by five seasons in which he won four American League ERA crowns. Yawkey did not force Collins to trade talent for talent. He provided his general manager the opportunity to toss significant monetary compensation into his deals to land superior players. The result in 1934 was a .500 record, marking the first time the team broke even since Babe Ruth, who was now approaching the end of his career, was still wearing a Red Sox uniform.

Yawkey understood when he bought the team that the road to contention could not be achieved at breakneck speed. The machine required to reach that destination had to be constructed one piece at a time. The result was steady improvement as the shrewd Collins used the owner's money to place accomplished veterans in the lineup and rotation. Among those that hurried the transformation was future Hall of Fame shortstop Joe Cronin, who was named player-manager in 1935. Cronin, who was acquired from the collapsing Washington Senators for $225,000 and weak-hitting infielder Lyn Lary, was an anomaly among major-league shortstops as a premier run producer, a doubles machine that arrived having exceeded 100 RBIs in five consecutive seasons. He guided and slugged the Sox to their first over-.500 finish since 1918 as Grove and Wes Ferrell combined to win 45 games. Even some of the holdovers from the bad old days were blossoming. Outfielder Roy Johnson, who had experienced the 114-loss season in 1932, had become a remarkably consistent and productive .300 hitter.

The Red Sox were steadily adding talent. They now boasted enough strong players to maintain respectability. But it seemed the Live Ball Era was passing them by. They still lacked the sluggers that had transformed the Yankees into perennial champions and had made other clubs competitive. Not one Red Sox player aside from Ruth in 1919 had hit more than 18 home runs in a season through 1935. Given the friendly dimensions of Fenway Park, one figured Boston would boast a distinct advantage if its lineup featured more home-run hitters.

Enter Jimmie Foxx. Collins was familiar with Foxx from their time together with the Athletics, but it didn't take an insider to know all about The Beast. Foxx had won successive Most Valuable Player awards in 1932 and 1933 while averaging an absurd 166 RBIs in those two seasons. He had led the American League in home runs three of the four years previous to the thievery perpetrated by the Red Sox in exchange for catcher George Savino, who never reached the majors, and pitcher Gordon Rhodes, who was on the tail end of a forgettable career. The obvious key to the deal was the $150,000 Yawkey tossed into it.

The reactions of Foxx and Philadelphia manager Connie Mack to the swap, which the *Boston Globe* deemed the most important in baseball history, could be charted on the opposite ends of the emotional spectrum. Mack was devastated. He referred to the tough times he experienced after the breakup of his dominant teams of the early 1910s. "Well, Jimmie's gone," Mack lamented. "After this I'm right back where I started. I'm giving no reasons [for letting Foxx go to the Red Sox]. They must be obvious or remain a mystery. I am not even going to discuss the team for next year. I am not in a position to do that now."

Sox slugger Jimmie Foxx early in his career with Boston.
WIKIMEDIA COMMONS

Foxx, on the other hand, was delirious. He had relented on contract negotiations to help the cash-strapped Athletics, who had been circling the drain for the past two seasons after winning two World Series titles. "Oh boy, what a break!" he exclaimed upon hearing of the trade. "Who said there isn't a Santa Claus?" Foxx then pulled a bat out of the closet. "This is going to do a lot of talking up in Boston next year. With good breaks, no injuries and any kind of start I believe I can break Babe Ruth's record for home runs in one season. Since I was going anyway, I'm glad it's the Red Sox. There's no other city to which I'd rather go than Boston. It's the most understanding baseball town in the country."[3]

Foxx didn't break Ruth's American League record of 60 home runs, but he destroyed the Babe's team mark of 29. He clobbered 41 and established a franchise record with 143 RBIs as well. The addition of Foxx helped attract 626,895 fans to Fenway, the team's largest attendance since 1909. The Red Sox certainly would have shattered their all-time mark had they not proved one of baseball's biggest disappointments. They took their first step back of the Yawkey era with a 74-80 record. Foxx received little support as Boston ranked seventh among eight teams in runs scored. The lack of offense proved frustrating for a premier pitching

Owner Tom Yawkey talks baseball with star pitcher Lefty Grove.
COURTESY OF THE BOSTON PUBLIC LIBRARY, LESLIE JONES COLLECTION

staff. The Sox hung around the pennant race with a 31-18 record in early June before collapsing.

Fans and baseball insiders began wondering why a franchise that could supposedly throw money around like Yawkey barely reached .500 in its best years while other owners struggled to make ends meet during the harshest economic times in American history. Yawkey's bunch in the late 1930s became known as the Gold Sox or the Millionaires. But the perception was not reality. The Red Sox owned the sixth-highest payroll in the American League when Yawkey assumed ownership in 1933. Six years later, when most of his premier players and most expensive purchases remained on the roster, they ranked fifth. His purchase of talent at exorbitant prices was not reflected by the team's payroll. The Yankees, even following Ruth's retirement, paid their players far more.[4]

The Yankees also continued to dominate, and the Red Sox seemed helpless in their pursuit. Their bats finally began to boom in 1937 as Foxx,

Lefty Grove helped bring the Sox back to life in the 1930s.
COURTESY OF THE BOSTON PUBLIC LIBRARY, LESLIE JONES COLLECTION

Sox owner Tom Yawkey and wife Elise enjoying the moment in 1938.

Cronin, and third baseman Pinkie Higgins, whom they had also acquired from the Athletics, combined for 63 home runs and 333 RBIs. But while they got hot, the Yankees sizzled. Boston won 11 of 14 in July and gained just a half-game. They went unbeaten over a 13-game span in late July and early August and slid just two games closer to the Bronx Bombers. By that time they were nine games out. Season over.

Deft acquisitions from the pool of minor leaguers, such as the one that landed brilliant second baseman Bobby Doerr in 1938, further bolstered the roster. Doerr helped the Red Sox finally emerge as a power that year as six players totaled 80 or more RBIs and the team finished second in the American League in runs scored and first in batting average at a lofty .299. Boston even flirted with pennant contention, remaining just 3½ games back on July 30. The Yankees embarked on a ridiculous 53-12 blitz during the meat of the season to blow away the competition. Boston finished a distant second.

Some Sox historians have offered that the inability of the Red Sox to maximize their veteran talent resulted from the inability of their veteran talent to play as a team and show respect to their manager. The roster was peppered with foul-tempered athletes who weren't about to recognize authority simply because it has been given. Such was particularly true regarding pitchers Grove and Ferrell, who resented that Cronin called pitches from the dugout. One example of player discontent occurred during a team slump late one season when Cronin arranged a morning workout to which he was the only player who showed up. Never mind that Cronin remained productive as a hitter through 1941. It wasn't his hitting that they complained about.[5]

Cronin was either calling the wrong pitches or simply didn't boast championship mound talent. The Red Sox generally finished around the middle of the American League pack in team earned-run average. Their starting staff aside from Grove would prove to be downright lousy in 1939. But the team would finish a strong second anyway, mostly because arguably the greatest hitter in baseball history had arrived on the Fenway scene.

CHAPTER SEVEN

The Growth of the Splendid Splinter

APRIL 20, 1939. OPENING DAY AT YANKEE STADIUM. SECOND INNING. First major-league at-bat for Red Sox rookie Ted Williams. Future Hall of Famer Red Ruffing on the mound. Strikeout.

The lanky 20-year-old known as The Kid did some thinking after returning to the dugout. "I know I can hit that guy," he said. And he proved it on his next trip to the plate, whacking a double off the center field wall. The man generally regarded as the greatest hitter in baseball history had provided a sneak preview of his talent and confidence against already the most storied franchise in the sport, one whose uniform he could very well have worn.[1]

The story began on August 30, 1918 when Theodore Samuel Williams was born in San Diego to a photographer and former US Cavalry soldier and a Mexican-American mother who dedicated her life to working with the Salvation Army. Wedded bliss could certainly not have described their marriage. The couple spent much time away from each other and their two sons, Ted and younger brother Danny, both of whom played baseball all day and all year at such venues as the North Park Playground in the welcoming climes of Southern California. The dedication of the older Williams boy caught the attention of playground director Rod Luscomb, who nurtured his talent and helped transform him into a wunderkind.

Williams emerged at Hoover High School as a brilliant hitter, but an equally dominant moundsman. He fanned opposing batters at a prolific pace, including 21 in one game against Redondo Beach, while wearing out opposing pitchers and catching the eyes of scouts from such clubs as the Yankees and Cardinals. That attraction heightened the maternal instincts of Williams's mother May, who understood that signing her son to a professional contract would require parental consent. And she had no intention of allowing young Ted to hang out without supervision with ballplayers, most of whom she considered drinkers and bums. So while her husband was negotiating a deal with the Yankees, she inked one with the Pacific Coast League San Diego Padres that would force her son to remain close to home. The contract stipulated that Ted could not be sent away for two years. More comforting for mom was that the Padres agreed to bring in veteran outfielder Cedric Durst to serve as a roommate and mentor.[2]

Unlike a slugger named Ruth a generation previous, Williams dropped his ambitions as a pitcher upon launching his professional career. He loved to hit and had proven his incredible talents at the plate not only at Hoover but also in American Legion and semipro competition. One early pitching appearance for the Padres, who were desperate to save other hurlers with a 12–8 deficit and back-to-back doubleheaders on the slate, resulted in Williams striking out the side, then allowing two home runs. That convinced him to focus solely on his hitting and outfield play. He hit .271 in 107 at-bats against premier minor-league pitching in his first professional season—not bad considering he had yet to graduate from high school.

Williams had yet to hit his first home run. But his raw talent was so obvious that *San Diego Evening Tribune* sportswriter Earl Keller suggested before the 1937 season to those willing to gamble on such things that Williams would emerge as the premier prospect in the sport. Keller offered the following:

> *If you want to make a little extra money to put in the old sock, bet it on young Teddy Williams to be taken as the outstanding Major League prospect after this year's Pacific Coast League baseball race is finished. . . . Williams will be heavier and in better condition than ever when the 1937 season rolls around. From his mother, we learn he has put on more than five pounds since the 1936 season ended.*[3]

That crystal ball proved quite accurate. Williams raised his batting average to .291 that year while exhibiting his burgeoning power stroke with 23 home runs. One newspaper cited him as the only left-handed batter to blast one over every right field fence in the Pacific Coast League. He was earning a reputation as another Joe DiMaggio, who had recently torn up the PCL before emerging as Ruth's replacement with the Yankees and a young superstar. One could already imagine that it would not be the last time Williams and DiMaggio would be compared. The debates over which was a superior ballplayer continue to rage.

The progression and promise of Williams inspired the Red Sox to sign him. They'd had their eye on Williams since 1936, when Eddie Collins scouted him, as well as future Hall of Fame second baseman Bobby Doerr, in San Diego. Among his Padres teammates was promising catcher Gene Desautels, who later recalled becoming convinced that Williams would achieve stardom.

"When [Collins] came out there . . . he asked me a lot of questions about Ted. 'What do you think of him?' I said, 'That kid is going to be a hell of a hitter.' I could tell, He could hit anything. I told him, 'He talks and thinks hitting every minute.' That's all Ted talked about. And he had the physical qualifications. He had the good forearms. Later, with Boston, he used to compare his muscles with Jimmie Foxx in the clubhouse. Ted would say, 'Hey, look at my skinny arms, and you with your muscular arms.' Jimmie would laugh and say, 'Why don't you put on some beef? Maybe you'll grow some muscles.' But Ted didn't need muscles. He could swing that bat and hit the fastball and pull it. . . . In San Diego he told me, 'I can pull anybody. I don't care how fast they are.' He'd say, 'Nobody is going to throw the ball by me.'"[4]

The Red Sox weren't ready to stick the 19-year-old Williams into their lineup in 1938, but the contract obligations that prevented him from moving away from San Diego for two years had been met. The bird was ready to fly—and he flew to Minneapolis to play for the Millers of the American Association. Williams had matured not only as a player but also as a person. He had come a long way from his days as gawky kid in San Diego who would howl annoyingly at movie theaters and pretend to swing a bat while jumping up and down on his bed at six in the morning. That maturity resulted in one of the greatest performances in minor-league history. He even claimed before the season that he knew he lacked the readiness to thrive at the major-league level despite what future Red Sox teammates described as anger that he didn't make the club out of spring training.

"I am not a good hitter," he told the *Minneapolis Star* with remarkably out-of-character modesty. "I am not a good hitter because I have plenty to learn at the plate. . . . Joe DiMaggio didn't make the major leagues until he was 21. . . . It would have been nice to have stuck with the Red Sox. It would have been swell to crash the major leagues at 19. But I'm not ready. I've got power, sure, and I can go and get 'em in that outfield, yes, but power and fly shagging aren't everything, I like to hit home runs but I've got to have a respectable batting average to go along with it. I'm going to learn how to get it."[5]

He sure got it—and then some. Williams won the American Association Triple Crown in 1938, batting .366 with 46 home runs and 142 RBIs while also topping one and all with 130 runs scored. That offensive explosion proved quite impressive for a teenager out of his San Diego comfort zone for the first time. That he would be promoted to the majors in 1939 was a foregone conclusion.

The Boston media went into a Williams frenzy as that season approached. The pressure was on. One must understand that he achieved much of his incredible batting success at a Minneapolis bandbox. The Red Sox sent him down in part to give him confidence in his ability to hit home runs, which the tiny park provided. The rational assumption was that blasting them out of far more spacious major-league stadiums would prove far more challenging.

That is, for mortal hitters. Not Ted Williams. He took baseball by storm in 1939, launching his big-league career with a nine-game hitting streak that included a two-homer game against Detroit. He continued to perform well as he learned American League pitching, raised his average over .300 on July 5 and kept it there the rest of the season. He embarked on a .468 blitz late that sent it soaring to .327 and finished the year there with 31 home runs and a league-best 145 RBIs. He finished fourth in the AL Most Valuable Player balloting behind DiMaggio, Foxx, and

Cleveland Indians ace right-hander Bob Feller despite playing in 29 more games and blasting more pitches over the fence while driving in more runs than Joltin' Joe.

The two factors weighing in DiMaggio's favor were that he had reached veteran status and played for the pennant-winning Yankees. Williams performed brilliantly as one of three Red Sox sluggers to top triple-figures in RBI, but it seemed nothing could vault their team atop the Bronx Bombers. Ruth had long since retired, Lou Gehrig was in a tragic battle for his very life, but the Big Apple boys rolled on. The Sox won more often head-to-head in 1939, including a five-game sweep at Yankee Stadium amid a 12-game winning streak. But that tear merely served to chop their deficit to six games. The Red Sox failed to sneak any closer the rest of the year.

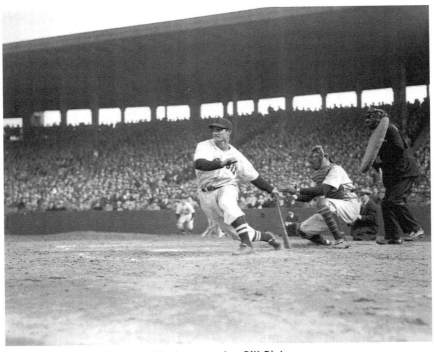

Bobby Doerr hitting in front of Yankees catcher Bill Dickey.
COURTESY OF THE BOSTON PUBLIC LIBRARY, LESLIE JONES COLLECTION

That gap lengthened as their record worsened before every major-league team was decimated by the loss of players to Uncle Sam in World War II. The cause was not an attack that finished second in runs scored in 1939 and 1940 and first the next year. It was poor starting rotations, led by an aging Lefty Grove, who won the ERA title in 1939, faded badly as he turned 40 in 1940, and retired after the following season. The staff was otherwise peppered with nonentities—nary an ace in the bunch. Mediocrities such as Jack Wilson, Fritz Ostermueller, Dick Newsome, and Mickey Harris headed staffs that finished near the bottom of the American League in team ERA and resulted in weakening Red Sox records and non-contention.

Williams could certainly never be blamed. But he developed his own issues with the fans and media. He became disenchanted with Fenway Park after his incredible rookie season, and owner Tom Yawkey was quick to submit to any Williams whim. The Splendid Splinter complained that at 400 feet from home plate, the right field fence was too distant. He added that he would find it beyond his desire to remain in Boston if the fence remained where it was. So Yawkey dutifully removed the bullpens from that spot and pulled the fences in 20 feet. The slugger spent the rest of his career bashing home runs into the area of Fenway that became known as Williamsburg.

Williams didn't send many baseballs there or over the Green Monster early in 1940. He was batting just .179 through eight games and, though his average soared, peaking at .382 in early June, he had just four home runs on June 8. His mistakes on defense, which was never a priority, were glaring. The local sportswriters and fans began to disparage his performance. Always sensitive to criticism, he reasoned that he was a perfectionist who was simply trying too hard and, furthermore, what right did media members who couldn't hit a baseball over a fence if they were standing in center field and it was tossed underhanded have to tell him how to hit? And when he heard boos cascading from the Fenway stands, he vowed never to acknowledge the fans as long as he remained in a Boston uniform. "That's it, I'm never going to tip my hat again," he said. And he didn't—not even when the thought crossed his mind as he rounded the bases after homering in his last major-league at-bat 20 years later. Indeed, his epic feud with the Boston media was launched in 1940.[6]

Williams was quite aware of his sensitivity, admitting to having "rabbit ears" as he listened for any boos or catcalls from the Fenway faithful. "[I was] never very coy, never very diplomatic," he said. "As a result I would get myself in a wringer. . . . I was impetuous, I was tempestuous. I blew up. Not acting but reacting. I'd get so damned mad, throw bats, kick the columns in the dugout so that sparks flew, tear out the plumbing, knock out the lights, damn near kill myself. Scream. I'd scream out my own frustration."[7]

Neither Boston fans nor Williams expressed much frustration in 1941. Part of his greatness as a thinking man's hitter—he was in the process of seven straight seasons (before and after his war service) in which he led the American League in on-base percentage—was developing a daily routine. He had settled into one by that year that started with a 6:00 a.m. fishing trip at Sunset Lake along with teammate Charlie Wagner, followed by the swinging of a bat or broomstick in the clubhouse around noon as he began preparation for 3:00 p.m. games (Fenway did not host a night game until 1947). Williams spent hours daily mimicking his swing, sometimes with a hairbrush in front of a mirror. He even took extra batting practice after games.

While other major leaguers were out drinking and carousing, Williams would eat a quick dinner and take in a western at the theater. He believed that boozing weakened body and mind, as well as his focus on hitting. During his first two years in the majors he had memorized tendencies and repertoires of American League pitchers, pored over box scores, and made friends with umpires to gain information from them about AL hurlers.[8]

Williams was driven to greatness and it all came to fruition in 1941, a season many consider the finest ever achieved by a major-league hitter. Nobody had broken the .400 barrier since Rogers Hornsby in 1925. It seemed that batting averages that high were part of the last vestiges of a bygone era. But Williams reached .400 on May 25 during a 23-game hitting streak in which he hit an even more ridiculous .489 and continued to flirt with the magic number the rest of the year. He appeared

Ted Williams and his famous uppercut during batting practice before Opening Day in 1956.
COURTESY OF THE BOSTON PUBLIC LIBRARY, LESLIE JONES COLLECTION

destined for immortality when he reached .413 in mid-September, but a mini-slump lowered his mark to .400 with a season-ending double-header looming against the Athletics in Philadelphia. With the Red Sox playing for nothing but pride, Williams was offered the option of sitting out to ensure he would make history, but his own pride would not allow it.

He had much to think about on the evening of September 27, the night before his date with destiny at Shibe Park. He felt antsy sitting around the Ben Franklin Hotel, so he took a three-hour walk around the City of Brotherly Love with clubhouse man Johnny Orlando, who stopped occasionally for a hard drink while Williams drank a soft one outside. "I kept thinking about the thousands of swings I had taken to prepare myself," Williams said years later. "I had practiced and practiced.

I kept saying to myself, 'You are ready.' I went to the ballpark the next day more eager to hit than I had ever been."[9]

Williams was certainly ready physically, mentally, and emotionally. In the opener, he singled to start the second inning, homered to open in the fifth, singled in the sixth, and singled in the seventh. He added a single and double in his first two at-bats in the nightcap and finished the season at .406, a mark that would forever remain a symbol of incredible achievement. The greatest hitters in baseball history, including such sweet swingers as Rod Carew and George Brett, have flirted with .400, but could not maintain the pace.

Yet despite the historic season, Williams again finished behind DiMaggio in the Most Valuable Player voting. The unfairness of the balloting that has always been tilted toward those that played for pennant winners in a most individual sport reared its ugly head. Williams owned an on-base percentage more than 100 points ahead of DiMaggio, batted 51 points higher, accrued 71 more walks, scored 13 more runs, and hit seven more homers. But DiMaggio was more popular with the media and he performed yet again for the American League champion.

Meanwhile, an event thousands of miles away from Boston and New York rocked baseball, America, and the world. The Japanese bombing of Pearl Harbor on December 7 sent many players packing to fight overseas. Williams had an out—he was a sole supporter of his divorced mother—and he indeed played ball in 1942. He was criticized by some as a coward for not joining the battle as he captured the first of his two Triple Crowns while also leading the league in every major statistical category.

Williams soon proved his patriotism. Though he never fought in combat, he spent the next three years training to be a Navy and Marine Corps pilot, eventually teaching others as a flight and gunnery instructor. The Red Sox languished in mediocrity as stars such as Williams, Doerr, and emerging infielder Johnny Pesky fulfilled their military duties. But Fenway would certainly be rocking when they returned in 1946.

CHAPTER EIGHT

The Championship, the Choice, and the Choke

PERHAPS THE PLANETS WERE ALIGNED JUST RIGHT FOR THE RED SOX in 1946. It wasn't simply that their premier players had returned from overseas. The same could be said for teams throughout Major League Baseball, though Boston boasted more premier everyday talent than most of those clubs.

The magical year in Beantown was the result of catching lightning in more than one bottle. They fleeced the Tigers in a trade that summoned slugging first baseman Rudy York for nonentity infielder Eddie Lake. All York did was drive in 117 runs and compile an on-base percentage of .371. They reaped the rewards of a 20-win year and the last strong effort from Tex Hughson before he faded prematurely into obscurity. They benefitted from a 25-victory season from fellow starter Dave "Boo" Ferriss before he too dropped off the face of the baseball earth.

Not that the Boston dominance in 1946 was driven strictly by fortunate circumstances. Williams, Doerr, and Pesky proved that their three-year absence had subtracted nothing from their skills. Outfielder Dom DiMaggio returned more productive than ever as he launched in earnest a career as a seven-time All-Star obscured only by playing in the shadow of his legendary brother. The result of everything breaking right was that Boston led the American League in runs scored, doubles, triples, batting average, on-base percentage, slugging percentage, and total bases.

Sluggers Rudy York (left) and Bobby Doerr pose during the 1946 World Series.
COURTESY OF THE BOSTON PUBLIC LIBRARY, LESLIE JONES COLLECTION

The pennant race was over before spring turned to summer. The Red Sox surged to one of the greatest starts in baseball history. A 15-game winning streak in late April and early May that remains a franchise-best raised their record to 21-3 and placed them 5½ games ahead of the pack. A 12-1 blitz launched two weeks later bolstered their mark to 41-9 and pushed them 10 games ahead more than three weeks before Independence Day. Game, set, match.

Neither the Red Sox nor Williams arrived at the World Series with optimum momentum. A six-game losing streak in September pushed back the pennant clinching. Williams slumped a bit down the stretch, the victim of an elbow ailment and stung by reports that the Red Sox were considering swapping him to the Yankees for Joe DiMaggio. It was believed that general manager Eddie Collins and manager Joe Cronin had grown frustrated at Williams's refusal to spray the ball to left field, even in the face of dramatic shifts implemented by Indians manager Lou Boudreau that placed three infielders on the right side. Trade rumors persisted despite front office denials.

Such were not the preferred circumstances as the Red Sox awaited a showdown against the St. Louis Cardinals and the franchise's first World Series since 1918. And, in the end, Williams, in what proved to be his only shot at a championship, dragged the team down to defeat. While Doerr, Dom DiMaggio, and particularly York proved themselves productive against everyone but frustratingly tantalizing southpaw Harry Brecheen, who won three games, Williams managed just five measly singles in an epic seven-game battle with no home runs and just one RBI. He slammed only one hit after the Sox had taken a 3–2 series lead and went 0-for-4 with the title on the line in Game 7. Those failures proved devastating for a player as intense and proud as Williams, whose frustration reached a peak in the eighth inning of the finale when he popped out with two out and the winning run on second. Then St. Louis star Enos "Country" Slaughter scored the clincher on a daring dash from first to home on a double, after which Pesky was criticized for holding onto the ball too long before firing it to the plate.

"I'm the goat," Pesky told reporters. "It's my fault. I'm to blame. I couldn't hear anybody hollering at me [to throw the ball] above the noise of the crowd. I gave Slaughter at least six strides with that delay."[1]

The defeat stayed with Pesky. "It was a sad, sad experience," he said years later. "Believe me. That was the all-time low for all of us. I remember looking over at Williams and, boy, he was really down. He was almost in tears. He might have even shed a tear or two. . . . To this day, I feel we had a better ballclub than the Cardinals."[2]

They didn't in 1947. They did not even have a better ballclub than the Yankees or Tigers. Boston finished third that season due greatly to the downfall of York, whose sudden failures proved so monumental that he was dispatched to the White Sox for nonentity first baseman Jake Jones in mid-June. Jones started off with a bang in a doubleheader against Chicago, slamming a home run in the opener and a game-winning grand slam in the nightcap. But he faded quickly.

BASEBALL DIGEST

DAVE FERRISS
Boston Red Sox

Dave "Boo" Ferriss enjoyed great success for the Sox in 1946 and beyond before fading.

York never rebounded. His alcohol problem reared its ugly head often, including one time in late April when he had to be rescued from a hotel room littered with liquor bottles after falling asleep with a lit cigarette in his hand and causing a fire. It was not the first time that had happened.[3]

Also damaging in 1947 were less productive seasons from Doerr and Pesky, and, most significantly, a predictable collapse of the starting staff. Ferriss proved particularly disappointing as the team ERA jumped nearly a half-point from 1946 and ranked a woeful sixth in the American League. But it was not entirely their fault. Ferriss, Hughson, and Mickey Harris all suffered from arm injuries that affected their performances. The Red Sox utilized 13 different starting pitchers that season.

A loss to lowly Washington on September 28 proved to be the last game Joe Cronin spent in a Boston uniform. After 14 years at the helm—including 12 as a player-manager—he was promoted to general manager. He and Yawkey both agreed to hire veteran skipper Joe McCarthy, who had never suffered through a losing season as manager of the Cubs and Yankees from 1926 to 1946 and had guided those teams to nine pennants and seven World Series crowns. So accomplished was McCarthy that Yawkey made him an offer he couldn't refuse—an annual salary of $100,000.

McCarthy came with more baggage than he stuffed his clothes into for his move to Boston. He brought with him a reputation as oversensitive to media criticism and a difficult manager for pitchers who yearned to know the exact date of their next start. He was also far more of a disciplinarian than Cronin and could be more difficult for pitchers who preferred a strict routine. Ace Mel Parnell stated that rather than abide by a strict rotation, McCarthy would inform pitchers that they would be starting that day by placing a ball under their cap in the clubhouse. Parnell understood the reasoning behind it. McCarthy did not want pitchers worrying about their next start the night before and allowing it to affect their sleep. And though the policy caused some consternation, McCarthy was generally more organized than his predecessor. He was widely liked and respected.

"Joe McCarthy was the best man I ever played for," Pesky said. "Joe was a very quiet man . . . if something happened, he would call you over, like a teacher you fall in love with in school. That was his kind of approach to the players. He wouldn't say, 'I want you to do this,' he'd say, 'Can I suggest this to you?'... McCarthy knew more baseball than any other man I ever saw. But there were some guys who didn't respond to Joe."[4]

Among them was Hughson, who was highly critical of McCarthy, recalling him as an alcoholic who mistreated ballplayers. But the new manager certainly lit a fire under the 1948 Red Sox. So did an infusion of talent such as slugging infielder Vern Stephens, who was traded from the Browns for money and six players who had achieved nothing upon their departure. Stephens, who drove in a team-high 137, teamed with Williams and Doerr for 375 RBIs and helped Boston lead the league in batting average, on-base percentage, and runs scored.

The result was a bunch that bashed its way into contention. Along with the Indians and Yankees, the Red Sox became embroiled in one of the most heated pennant races ever after a terrible start. A three-game sweep by Cleveland in early May dropped them 5½ games off the pace, and they stood more than 10 games back after falling to 15-24 on June 2. They rebounded to remain in the periphery of first place, cooled off to drop back to .500, then sizzled. They got hot with a 10-4 run, then caught fire during a marathon 16-game homestand. The Red Sox won 13 in a row, including a revenge sweep of Cleveland, to vault into the lead as their often-maligned pitching staff allowed one run or fewer in seven of those games.

The rest of the season boiled down to a nip-and-tuck battle with the Indians and Yankees. The Red Sox knocked out the Bronx Bombers on October 2 but remained one game behind Cleveland. They defeated the Yankees again to close out the regular season and when Detroit battered Indians ace Bob Feller that afternoon, the first playoff in American League history was set. The Tribe and Sox were to battle for the crown in Boston the following day. Beantown was psyched for a possible World Series showdown between the Red Sox and crosstown Braves.

McCarthy faced a myriad of palatable choices to start that game. Parnell had proven himself the premier pitcher on a deep staff with a 15-8 record and 3.14 ERA. Jack Kramer, who had arrived with Stephens in the thievery of the Browns, won 18 of 23 decisions to achieve the best winning percentage in the American League. Joe Dobson won 16 games. Neither Kramer nor Dobson, both of whom had pitched against the Yankees, were at full strength, so Parnell seemed the likely choice.

But rather than select any of them, McCarthy pegged part-time starter Denny Galehouse to pitch the game that would decide whether the Red Sox would remain alive for a championship. Galehouse owned an 8-8 record with a high 1.442 WHIP. He had been inconsistent late in the season, making the move a stretch. His teammates were stunned. Perhaps the most surprised was the southpaw Parnell, whom McCarthy had originally chosen but was spurned because the wind was blowing out to left field and the Indians boasted a lineup featuring right-handed sluggers Boudreau, Ken Keltner, and Joe Gordon. The change of starters left even Galehouse in a state of nervous shock.

"I thought of Denny Galehouse as nothing but a relief pitcher," said catcher Matt Batts. "When McCarthy picked him to start that game, the whole club was upset about it. The whole 25 ballplayers."[5]

The unexpected certainly affected his performance. Galehouse, who was 36 and nearing the end of a nondescript career, blew an opportunity for positive immortality in the biggest start of his life when he allowed a home run to the American League Most Valuable Player Boudreau in the first inning and a three-run blast to Keltner in the fourth. The Red Sox never recovered in an 8–3 defeat. Ironically, Indians starter Gene Bearden, who tossed a five-hit complete game, was a left-hander. Parnell later stated that the decision to pitch Galehouse demoralized the team. And after the game, McCarthy admitted to Parnell that he had made a mistake.

The players lost a bit of respect for McCarthy after that bungle and perhaps it showed early in the 1949 season as the Red Sox got off to another slow start, falling under .500 and 12 games out of first place on Independence Day. But the power combo of Doerr, Stephens, and Williams, who won his second Most Valuable Player award in four years, proved more potent than ever with 100 home runs and 527 RBIs between them. Stephens and Williams tied for the league lead by driving in 159 apiece while leadoff sparkplug Dom DiMaggio continued his vain attempt to emerge from his brother's shadow by raising his on-base percentage over .400 and scoring 126 runs. The Red Sox averaged nearly six runs a game. Meanwhile, Parnell and Ellis Kinder authored one of the best seasons by a Boston pitching tandem in decades, winning 48 games and compiling a 3.04 ERA between them.

The result of the hitting prowess and strong starting pitching was a second-half tear. A win at Yankee Stadium that launched an eight-game winning streak began a 37-10 onslaught that pushed Boston to within 2½ games of first place New York. The Sox hung around but remained three games out on September 11. That's when they embarked on an 11-game blitz that pushed them one game ahead of the Yankees. One victory in a season-ending two-game series in the Big Apple would give Boston the pennant and a shot at their first World Series title in 31 years.

Parnell had a shot at pitching the 1948 debacle into the dustbin of history. And it appeared he would do just that when he blanked the

A young Ted Williams and Bobby Doerr at Fenway in 1939.
COURTESY OF THE BOSTON PUBLIC LIBRARY, LESLIE JONES COLLECTION

Bombers for three innings and his team scratched out three runs in the third on five walks and a single to make it 4–0. But Parnell could not stand prosperity and he quickly gave all the runs back and departed the mound in favor of Dobson, who shut down the Yankees. The score remained tied into the bottom of the eighth when fading outfielder Johnny Lindell—not DiMaggio or Yogi Berra or Phil Rizzuto or Tommy Henrich—played the role of hero. He blasted a home run to win the battle and place New York in a flat-footed tie with one game remaining.

Nearly 70,000 fans packed The House That Ruth Built for the Sunday showdown between 20-game winners Kinder and Yankees ace right-hander Vic Raschi. The latter simply outpitched the former in an epic duel in which it appeared into the eighth inning that a first-inning leadoff triple and run by Rizzuto would decide the outcome. But Parnell, who had replaced Kinder, proved that either he was tired or not one to rise to the occasion and took another beating. He allowed a Henrich home run and single, then Hughson poured gasoline on the fire, giving

Ted Williams blasts one at Fenway in 1946.
COURTESY OF THE BOSTON PUBLIC LIBRARY, LESLIE JONES COLLECTION

up a three-run double to Jerry Coleman to stretch the deficit to 5–0. The Sox finally got to Raschi in the ninth on a two-run triple by Doerr, but they were soon back in the clubhouse lamenting a second straight excruciating finish to a season. Not only had they lost the pennant on the final day again, but a relationship with the Yankees akin to that of a punching bag and boxer was beginning to strengthen. And it would remain a frustrating reality for more than a half-century.

The defeat had Boston fans and the media second-guessing McCarthy, who had removed Kinder for a pinch-hitter in the eighth. One can never predict outcomes, but had Kinder continued to mow down the Yankees, that Doerr triple would have won the game and the pennant. Kinder allowed his anger to fester during the train ride back to Boston. He confronted McCarthy, scolding him for his removal. Kinder later told *Boston Post* sportswriter Al Hirshberg, "Goddammit, if the old man had let me bat for myself that day we'd have won the pennant."[6]

The Boston faithful were growing tired of those failures. They had been waiting three decades to celebrate a championship. Little could most of them have imagined that they would be dead and buried before what would eventually be described as Red Sox Nation would have a chance to rejoice.

CHAPTER NINE

Pushing for Pumpsie

IT WAS SEPTEMBER 20, 1950. FROM A PURE BASEBALL STANDPOINT, that date was the beginning of the end for that era of Red Sox pennant contention. They began that day in third place, a mere half-game behind Detroit and one game in arrears of the Yankees (who else?). They were set to open a critical four-game road trip against two of the premier teams in the American League—Cleveland and New York.

The slugging Sox were outscored 30–9, dropping all of the games and destroying their season. They had remained alive after a doubleheader sweep to the Indians, but ace Mel Parnell didn't pitch like one in the Big Apple, again getting clobbered with title hopes on the line, and it was over. The hopes and dreams of the Red Sox and their fans had been dashed. The feeling was quite familiar.

There seemed little reason, however, that such an excursion, no matter how galling it proved to be, would end the Boston run of contention. One reason for optimism was the performance that season of first baseman Walt Dropo, who earned Rookie of the Year honors by batting .322 with 34 home runs and 144 RBIs and a .583 slugging percentage second on the team only to Ted Williams. Who knows? Perhaps the Sox would have won the pennant had the Splendid Splinter not lost two months to an elbow injury sustained when he slammed against the wall making a catch in the All-Star Game.

The sextet of Williams, Bobby Doerr, Vern Stephens, Dom DiMaggio, Johnny Pesky, and Dropo seemed destined to wreak havoc against American League pitchers for at least a few more years. The .302 team

Sox shortstop Johnny Pesky in a thoughtful pose in 1951.
COURTESY OF THE BOSTON PUBLIC LIBRARY, LESLIE JONES COLLECTION

batting average in 1950 still ranks as the best in franchise history. Every starter hit at least .294—and utility man Billy Goodman amazingly topped them all at .354. Boston's 1,027 runs scored were the most of any major-league team since 1936 and has not been topped since. The relentless attack appeared certain to overcome a perennially mediocre pitching staff for the near future.

Appearances can be deceiving. Dropo slumped badly and was shipped to the Tigers in 1952 along with the aging, fading Pesky. Doerr slumped in 1951, hurt his back, and retired to his Oregon farm. Stephens, who had led the American League in runs batted in for two consecutive seasons, injured his knee and was never the same. Under new manager Lou Boudreau and with Williams off fighting in Korea, the Sox scored nearly 400 fewer runs in 1952 than they had just two years earlier. The result was their first under-.500 record, aside from the roster-ravaging war years, since 1936.

Though owner Tom Yawkey and his management team could hardly be blamed for injuries and surprising drops in production, another issue reared its ugly head and contributed to a period of mediocrity that lasted throughout the 1950s and beyond. And that was an unwillingness to ride the tide of integration and sign African-American ballplayers, many of whom were contributing greatly to major-league teams. Future Hall of Famers such as Jackie Robinson, Larry Doby, Satchel Paige, Roy Campanella, Monte Irvin, Willie Mays, Hank Aaron, and Ernie Banks had earned distinctions as baseball superstars while the notoriously racist Yawkey steadfastly refused to figuratively remove the "Whites Only" sign from the home team clubhouse at Fenway Park.

Yawkey defended his inaction by dredging up the name of longtime baseball commissioner Kenesaw Mountain Landis, who unwaveringly maintained segregation in the sport for many years, but who claimed a year before his death in 1944, three years before Robinson joined the Brooklyn Dodgers, that no such ban existed. Baseball historian Ken Burns cited the Red Sox owner as referring to Landis as an "implacable foe of integration who had done more than any other to perpetuate baseball's color line."[1]

The Red Sox held what has been described as sham tryouts of black players, including one of Robinson in 1945. Mays and 1950 National League Rookie of the Year Sam Jethroe, who integrated the Boston Braves, also worked out at Fenway. Evidence mounted that the Red Sox had no intention of signing an African American. Manager Pinky Higgins in 1955 was quoted as confirming that "there will be no niggers on this ball club as long as I have anything to say about it." And Robinson years later called Yawkey "one of the most bigoted guys in baseball" and offered after his so-called tryout, "It burns me up to come fifteen hundred miles to have them give me the runaround. . . . Not for one minute did we think the tryout was sincere."[2]

Then-manager Eddie Collins claimed that his team had dutifully scouted African-American players, but that nary a one was good enough to wear a Red Sox uniform. Reports surfaced that upon seeing Robinson working out at Fenway, general manager Joe Cronin yelled out "get those niggers off the field!"[3]

Team after team relented and integrated while the Red Sox maintained their all-white roster and mediocrity. Boston would not finish any closer than 11 games out of first place until the Impossible Dream season of 1967 as attendance plummeted. Even the return of Williams from military service in mid-May could not help the Sox salvage a miserable 1954, though the steal of a deal that netted consistent slugging outfielder Jackie Jensen from Washington allowed the team to remain over .500 as the decade progressed. But while black players such as Doby, Luke Easter, and Minnie Minoso helped keep the Indians and White Sox in contention and the Yankees received contributions from Elston Howard, the Red Sox refused to sign or promote talent that could have transformed them from also-ran to World Series threat. It seemed those they played on their minor-league teams were doomed to stay there.

Among them was an Oklahoma-born outfielder named Elijah Jerry Green Jr. who had moved to Oakland during his youth and was better known as Pumpsie. The Red Sox had purchased his contract in 1955 during a season in which he hit .319 with 12 home runs for Class C Stockton. Racial prejudice had prevented Green from ascending the ranks at a pace worthy of his production. Green, despite a keen eye at the plate that resulted in an encouraging on-base percentage, leveled off statistically after signing with the Sox. But the growing outcry against Yawkey and his refusal to bring black ballplayers to the big leagues finally contributed to a steady rise through the organization. Green rose to the occasion when invited to spring training in 1959, batting .444 with three home runs and earning top-rated rookie honors in a vote of sportswriters.[4]

"That was the best spring I've had in my life," recalled Green, whose brother Cornell would emerge as an All-Pro safety for the NFL Dallas Cowboys. "The best ball I ever played in my life. I had the whole package. I was a shoo-in. . . . I didn't know I was that good." But the same Higgins that once declared profanely he would never manage a black player had apparently not rid himself of such prejudices and returned Green to the minors. The Boston media was incensed. So was the local chapter of the National Association for the Advancement of Colored People, which screamed for an investigation of Yawkey and his practices of racial discrimination.[5]

That Green thrived at the plate in spring training was amazing given the obstacles he was forced to overcome. He had been turned away at the team motel in Phoenix, forcing a move to another 17 miles out of town. Sox publicity director Jack Malaney claimed to the media that the Safari, where the other players stayed, had simply run out of rooms with all the tourists in town. The sad circumstances inspired *Boston Globe* writer Milton Gross to offer the following:

From night to morning, the first Negro player to be brought to spring training by the Boston Red Sox ceases to be a member of the team he hopes to make as a shortstop. [Segregation] comes in a man's heart, residing there like a burrowing worm. It comes when a man wakes alone, eats alone, goes to the movies every night alone because there's nothing more for him to do and then, in Pumpsie Green's own words, "I get a sandwich and a glass of milk and a book and I read myself to sleep."[6]

Green performed at Triple-A Minnesota seemingly undaunted, though he later admitted that he would have preferred to play for his hometown Oakland Oaks of the Pacific Coast League rather than integrate the Red Sox. He batted .320 and scored 77 runs in just 98 games. Also displaying major-league talent was African-American pitcher Earl Wilson, who boasted a 10-1 record. One wondered at midseason how long the last-place Sox could keep Green and Wilson down and which one would be promoted first. Both questions were answered when Green was brought up on July 21 (Wilson arrived later that year and enjoyed a far more fruitful career, winning 22 games for Detroit in 1967 and helping that team win a World Series crown the following season).

Green joined his new teammates during a road trip, debuted as a pinch-runner, and was placed into the starting lineup a week later. He was batting .292 when he played in his first game at Fenway Park against Kansas City on August 4. Black Celtics superstar Bill Russell greeted him upon his arrival at the ballpark. Green received a phone call in the dugout from long-since-retired Jackie Robinson. Ted Williams treated him warmly. And black Boston fans, many of whom had switched allegiances to major-league teams that had embraced integration, besieged Fenway. Management roped off a large section of center field for African-American patrons who had plenty to cheer about. He received a standing ovation as he stepped to the plate as the leadoff hitter. Green knew he could not let the fans down. So he gave himself a pep talk.

"I said, 'Pumpsie, one thing you want to do is you want to hit the ball. You do not want to strike out and have to walk all the way back to the dugout after receiving a standing ovation,'" he recalled. Soon the crowd was rising to its feet again as Green bashed a triple off the namesake Monster.[7]

Green did not hit one over the Green Monster or any other home-run fence in baseball until September 7, but he ranked among the team's premier hitters for nearly a month, maintaining a .307 average in late August before a 0-for-24 swoon to end the season sent it reeling to .233. He would never again hit his way into an everyday spot in the lineup. And the Red Sox to at least some extent would continue to pay for the racist negligence of Yawkey and his management team during the early 1960s as the team suffered through its worst period since the post-Ruth era. They finished under .500 every year from 1959 to 1966 and even lost 100 games in 1965 for the first time in 33 years. It was no coincidence— and perhaps it was a bit of karma—that the Sox would not rise again until African-American stars such as George "Boomer" Scott and Reggie Smith were wearing their uniform.

CHAPTER TEN

Yaz and the Impossible Dream

THE LATE 1950S WERE YEARS OF HEARTACHE FOR RED SOX FANS, WHO were showing up to Fenway Park in dwindling numbers. Their beloved team was slowly descending from competitive to awful. Young phenoms such as shortstop Don Buddin, who was touted as the next Bobby Doerr, performed more like Bobby Kennedy upon his arrival in Boston.

Meanwhile, the immortal Ted Williams was on the verge of retirement. After playing his entire career with the Red Sox he famously homered in his last at-bat on September 28, 1960. That was among the few highlights of a season in which Boston bottomed out with a record of 65-89, their worst since 1933. A batting attack that not long before had terrorized American League pitching had finished sixth in runs scored, and a staff that had at least proven respectable ranked dead last in earned run average. A team that once boasted Williams and Doerr and Pesky and Stephens and DiMaggio now featured the likes of Buddin, Pete Runnels, Chuck Schilling, Gary Geiger, and Jim Pagliaroni.

Only one player brought a ray of sunshine to the gloom. And that was the man with a last name likely loved by Scrabble aficionados—Carl Yastrzemski. The son of a Polish potato farmer and Depression-era baseball prospect who had played his college ball at Merrimack College in North Andover, a mere half-hour drive from Boston, compiled ridiculous numbers in just two minor-league seasons. Yastrzemski batted .377 with 100 RBIs and a .472 on-base percentage at Class B Raleigh in 1958, placing him on a fast track to Fenway. He skyrocketed all the way to Triple-A Minneapolis the following season and hit .339. That he would

Carl Yastrzemski displays the form that made him one of the most popular players in franchise history.

carry the heavy burden of replacing Williams in the Red Sox lineup in 1961 had become a foregone conclusion. The emotional weight, which carried unrealistic fan expectations, proved overwhelming.

"They almost destroyed me," said Yastrzemski. "It got so after the first couple of games a base hit wasn't enough. I had to hit a home run and I wasn't a home-run hitter in those days. I was a spray hitter." So distraught had Yastrzemski become that he elicited the help of owner Tom Yawkey, who summoned Williams to come to the rescue. The legend flew to Boston to give the rookie a pep talk that had its desired results. Soon the fans began to understand the greatness of Yastrzemski as unique without making unfair comparisons.[1]

Good thing, too, because Yastrzemski was no Williams. The hitting talent of Hall of Famers can pale in comparison to that of Williams. Yastrzemski owned neither the power nor consistency of his predecessor. He hit 40 home runs in a season three times during one four-year stretch but otherwise never blasted more than 28. He retired with a quite mortal .285 career batting average. He managed more than 102 RBIs only in 1967 and 1969. He earned a spot in the Hall of Fame as much for his longevity as his typical annual statistics, as well as a toughness that legendary sportswriter Peter Gammons stated was at the highest level of any ballplayer he covered over nearly a half-century. Yastrzemski did everything well. He led the American League in doubles thrice and on-base percentage five times. He earned six Gold Gloves. And he made 18 All-Star Game appearances.

Yastrzemski took tremendous pride in his defense, particularly his ability to use the Green Monster to his advantage. He conquered the nuances of playing the only left field wall in baseball that made batters think twice about taking the extra base and turned doubles into singles. Boston sports columnist and author Dan Shaughnessy wrote the following about Yastrzemski's personal relationship with the most famous barrier in baseball:

There can be little doubt that Carl Yastrzemski was the master of Wall-ball defense . . . [He] had the coordination, the instincts, and the work ethic to make the Wall work for him. He was among the

American League's outfield assist leaders annually until baserunners learned to stop going for two when they clanged one off the Wall. Yaz could decoy better than any outfielder and routinely pretended he was ready to catch a ball that he knew was going to carom off the Wall. Sometimes this would make runners slow down or stop altogether.[2]

The all-around brilliance of Yastrzemski could not prevent the Red Sox from languishing near the bottom of the American League standings through the first six years of his career. Occasional offensive contributions by fellow Boston hitters such as Frank Malzone and Dick Stuart brought little hope to fans as the troubling attendance figures of the 1950s dropped to crisis proportions and had Yastrzemski considering asking Yawkey to trade him following the 1966 season. Even the influx of young hitting talent such as George Scott, Rico Petrocelli, and Tony Conigliaro in the mid-1960s did nothing to attract patrons. A terrible pitching staff that stood out like a sore thumb in an era of staunch hurlers made certain that Boston would finish light years out of first place. The Sox ranked among the bottom three in team ERA every year from 1960 to 1966, falling to the cellar in that statistic in the last of those seasons.

Nothing the Red Sox achieved in player personnel appeared destined to make a significant difference in 1967. The emergence of Scott allowed them to swap promising, but troubled first baseman Tony Horton to Cleveland for aging Gary Bell, who promised to add depth to a rotation desperately in need of it. Rookie outfielder Reggie Smith reached the big leagues but was not ready to fulfill his vast potential. One could not imagine the natural growth of younger Sox vaulting what had been a poor team for years into contention.

One bold move did appear destined to change the culture for better or for worse. And that was the hiring of Dick Williams as manager. Williams hopped on the carousel of 1960s skippers that had already featured Billy Jurges, Del Baker, Pinky Higgins, Johnny Pesky, Billy Herman, and Pete Runnels. The differences were vast between the managerial styles of Williams and Herman, who had been in charge in 1966 before a late firing.

The ouster of Herman was motivated by his negative relationship with Yastrzemski. The beginning of the end occurred when the former called for a team meeting to vote for a Red Sox captain, a job the latter knew he would get but did not want because of its hassles and the need to act as an intermediary between player requests and Yawkey. Yastrzemski was indeed voted captain. He began eliciting help from Herman, who soon told his star player to stop bugging him.

The mutual dislike intensified. Herman accused Yastrzemski in late September of loafing on the field. The manager was not alone in making that charge. Among those that confirmed such a reputation was former Yankees pitcher and author Jim Bouton, who wrote the following about Yastrzemski in his controversial 1969 book *Ball Four*:

> *I'm afraid Yastrzemski had a bit of dog in him. Always did, and people around baseball knew it all the time. When things are going good Yastrzemski will go all out. When things aren't going so well he'll give a half-ass effort. But he's got so much ability that the only thing you can do is put up with him.*[3]

Yastrzemski responded to the criticism in early September by issuing an ultimatum—either Herman was fired or he would demand to be dealt. Trade rumors were bandied about by the Boston media as the distracted Yastrzemski slumped. Yawkey had to decide between his star player and Herman—and the choice given the team's lack of talent was clear. He fired Herman on September 8 and replaced him with Runnels on an interim basis. The Red Sox played .500 ball under Runnels while Yastrzemski went on a tear at the plate, inspiring Yawkey to offer Runnels the job for 1967. But health concerns motivated him to turn it down. Soon Yawkey hired Williams to take over the club.

Herman had earned a reputation as a lax leader. He was almost too nice a guy for the job—issues with Yastrzemski notwithstanding. Players took advantage of the lack of rules, such as having no set curfew. They would party with women until early morning, then talk about the revelry in front of Herman on the team bus minutes later. The attitude of the club began to improve along with the realization that young talent such as Petrocelli, Scott, Conigliaro, and 1965 International League batting champion Joe Foy could help Yastrzemski make the Red Sox competitive. But it would take more of a disciplinarian to transform the sorry Sox into a contender.

That no-nonsense authoritarian was Williams, who had recently shown more than baseball acumen when he won big money on game shows *You Don't Say* and *Hollywood Squares*. He scrapped the job of captain and brought law and order to the clubhouse and beyond. He ordered that single players stay in a hotel. He summoned Ted Williams to work with the team during spring training, then angered him and inspired him to leave camp by interrupting one of the legend's bull sessions. Dick Williams didn't take anything from anyone. Williams battled complacency. He established a curfew and demanded the players stay in shape all year. Most impressed was new assistant coach Bobby Doerr.

"There's something in Dick's voice, his way," Doerr explained. "When he says, 'Be at the park at 9 o'clock,' you know you'd better be there. He doesn't have to rant and rave. There's no falseness about him. Players soon sense falseness in a manager. Managing is like hitting—you either have it or you don't. Williams has it. There's no tension on his club . . . but he has the authority. The players respect him."[4]

Only 8,000 fans showed up for the opener at frigid Fenway. After winning six of seven against weak competition, the Sox foundered, falling two games under .500 and seven out of first place in late May. They began to play better, but a five-game losing streak in early July punctuated by a three-game sweep in Detroit sent their record reeling to 40-39 and pushed them seven games back again. Then the Red Sox got red-hot. They embarked on a stunning 10-game winning streak in which emerging ace Jim Lonborg won three decisions. Yastrzemski launched the tear with a four-game explosion in which he batted .500 with three home runs and nine RBIs. Boston outscored its opponents, 67–26, during the blitz.

Perhaps the greatest pennant race in baseball history was on. Boston, Detroit, Minnesota, and Chicago jockeyed for position. A 10-14 slide placed the Sox in fourth place, 3½ games behind the sizzling Twins. They suffered another blow on August 18 when a fastball by Angels pitcher Jack Hamilton struck Conigliaro in the eye, wiped out his season, and threatened his career. But a 7-0 run in which right-hander Gary Bell won twice catapulted them into a flat-footed tie for the top. They remained at least within one game of the lead the rest of the season.

Meanwhile, Yastrzemski was in a hitting frenzy. He slammed two home runs to help complete a three-game sweep of the Senators. He slugged a game-tying blast in the ninth inning of a critical win in Detroit. He bashed four hits in a defeat of Cleveland that started a season-ending 10-game hitting streak. He clobbered a three-run homer to put away the Twins and set up a virtual three-way tie for first place with Detroit and Minnesota with one game remaining. The Tigers required a sweep of the Angels in their doubleheader on the final day to force a playoff.

The battle in Boston featured 20-game winners Lonborg and Twins veteran Dean Chance. Twins heavy hitters Tony Oliva and Harmon Killebrew drove in runs early to put the Red Sox on the ropes. But a daring leadoff bunt in the sixth by Lonborg followed by successive hits brought up Yastrzemski, who had already singled and doubled. He had to resist temptation to try to unload the loaded bases. He repeated to himself to go for the single rather than the homer and achieved his goal to tie the game. Chance soon fell apart on the mound and his teammates joined in with mishaps in the field.

Soon Lonborg was inducing hitting machine Rod Carew to ground into a double play in the ninth and clinching the win as the Fenway faithful—in an era before it was security personnel's job to stop such an invasion—poured onto the field. Many made a beeline toward Lonborg, the hero of the day. Though the incursion from the stands had Red Sox hearts racing a bit faster and they sought in vain to escape to the comfort of the clubhouse, they also appreciated the joyous and raucous reaction. It was returned in kind by the players. "Jubilation," Petrocelli said. "The fans running on the field—you could see in their eyes the joy and excitement of a team going to the World Series. That team stole the hearts of the fans."[5]

To be chronologically precise, the team had not yet clinched a berth in the Fall Classic. Detroit had won the first game of its doubleheader.

Ace pitcher Jim Lonborg played a key role in the surprising run to the pennant in 1967.

Two-time all-star Rico Petrocelli played his entire career in Boston.
NATIONAL BASEBALL HALL OF FAME AND MUSEUM

The celebration had to wait as the players huddled around a radio to listen to the nightcap. Final score: Angels 8, Tigers 5.

"Every time the Tigers made an out, we cheered," Petrocelli recalled. "Then the Angels would score a run, and we'd think it was us. The final out, we jumped up, hugging, opening champagne. Corks were popping."[6]

The Impossible Dream was now a reality. Yastrzemski, who hit a preposterous .526 over the final two weeks of the season, had gone 4-for-4 with the pennant on the line. It has been offered that Red Sox Nation was born that day. Cars honked on the streets around Fenway. Kenmore Square was in gridlock. The Sox and their fans were delirious. But the breaking of the Curse of the Bambino had yet to be achieved. That would require a World Series defeat of a St. Louis Cardinals team that had won 101 games and featured such future Hall of Fame talent as outfielder Lou Brock, first baseman Orlando Cepeda, and pitchers Steve Carlton and Bob Gibson.

While Williams had to wait until Game 2 to pitch his ace Lonborg and was forced to send Jose Santiago to the mound, Cardinals manager Red Schoendienst had an array of choices to start the opener. One-year wonder Dick Hughes won 16 games and led the National League in WHIP.

Nelson Briles boasted the lowest ERA on the team. Carlton and Gibson both owned 2.98 earned run averages. But Schoendienst understood that Gibson boasted the best stuff of the bunch and announced him as the Game 1 starter. He made the right decision. Gibson began making his mark as one of the greatest big-game hurlers in baseball history by throwing a complete-game six-hitter in which the only run he allowed, oddly, was a home run by Santiago.

Gibson had set the tone. The 1967 World Series would be remembered forever as a personal battle between Gibson and Lonborg. The Boston ace outdid his counterpart with a one-hit shutout in Game 2. Gibson blanked the Sox in a Game 4 rout in which Santiago was knocked out in the first inning. The Red Sox were on the verge of a Fall Classic defeat, but Lonborg stymied St. Louis in Game 5 and a four-homer effort in Game 6, including two from Petrocelli, sent the series to a seventh and deciding game at Fenway. For the first time, it would be Gibson vs. Lonborg. The latter would be pitching on only two days' rest. The baseball world awaited the showdown. So inspired was *Boston Globe* sportswriter Bud Collins at what a Boston team that entered the season as a 100-1 shot to win the World Series had accomplished that he wrote, "the Fenway Phoenixes have risen from the ashes so many times that they must be on pulleys, like Peter Pan."[7]

Stated Williams as one and all awaited Game 7: "They can call it destiny, luck, ability, or a combination of all three. Whatever it is, I hope it lasts one more day. . . . My lineup is simple. Lonborg and champagne."[8]

There would be poor pitching from the former and none of the latter. Lonborg allowed two home runs, including two to his counterpart, and was removed in the seventh after allowing seven runs while Gibson was firing a three-hit complete game. Lonborg left to a standing ovation from

Shortstop and thrid baseman Rico Petrocelli brought steady production in twelve full seasons with Boston, peaking as a home run hitter from 1969 to 1971.

the Fenway fans. He had simply run out of gas. "Jim's heart was there, but his arm wasn't," concluded Yastrzemski.[9]

Yastrzemski's heart and bat were there throughout the series. He ended his remarkable season on the same roll in which he began it by batting .400 with three home runs. He had finished the regular season batting .326 with 44 home runs and 121 RBIs as the last American League Triple Crown winner until Tigers slugger Miguel Cabrera achieved it in 2012. And though Yastrzemski would capture an American League batting title in 1968, bash 40 home runs in each of the next two years, remain a superstar for a decade beyond, and land in the Hall of Fame, he would always be remembered most for making the Impossible Dream a reality.

CHAPTER ELEVEN

The Tragic Tale of Tony C.

RARELY IS A FIT BETWEEN BALLPLAYER AND TEAM, BETWEEN BALL-player and fan base, between ballplayer and city, so perfect that his story becomes almost dreamlike, as if it belongs in a movie script rather than real life. But the line between beautiful dream and reality was indeed blurred for Tony Conigliaro. That is, until it turned tragic in the blink of an eye. His Disney fairytale descended into a Stephen King horror story on a warm August night at Fenway Park in 1967—Friday the 18th.

The Battle of the Bulge was raging thousands of miles away when Anthony Richard Conigliaro was born on January 7, 1945 in Revere, a mere 17-minute drive from Boston. He and younger brother Billy, who managed to forge a fleeting major-league career, including a three-year stint with the Red Sox, became obsessed with the sport, which was taught to them by their uncle Vinnie Martelli. The older Conigliaro brother would practice his batting stroke until his hands bled. So advanced had he become as a hitter that he slugged a home run over the center field fence in his first at-bat for the Orient Heights Little League team.

Conigliaro also gained a fierce competitive spirit, though he received little experience in emotionally overcoming defeat. His talent played a huge role in the dominance of his teams. Meanwhile, scouts had taken notice of Conigliaro, who pitched and played shortstop in high school and American Legion ball. No wonder—his batting average hovered around .600 and he won 16 games for a team that won the Catholic Conference championship. The kid was a natural. Major-league bids poured

Slugger Tony Conigliaro was all smiles until a Jack Hamilton fastball slammed into his eye in 1967.
NATIONAL BASEBALL HALL OF FAME AND MUSEUM

in. After a workout at Fenway Park in 1962, he was offered a $20,000 bonus from Boston and signed it. Hometown boy makes good.[1]

Conigliaro had it all. He was talented, handsome, and just 18 years old. He was invited to Red Sox spring training in 1963 before being assigned to Class A Wellsville. Whether the organization underestimated his greatness or simply yearned to give him confidence, Conigliaro dominated pitching at that level. He batted .363 with 24 home runs, 42 doubles, and 74 RBIs.

So much for the minors. Boston manager Johnny Pesky, who lived on the same street as the Conigliaro family in Swampscott, brought the lanky young phenom with the sweet swing and powerful wrists back to spring training in Scottsdale in 1964. Conigliaro dazzled Pesky with his intensity and power, which he displayed in front of his parents when he blasted a bomb off Indians and future Red Sox right-hander Gary Bell. Visiting luminary Ted Williams was impressed with the stance and stroke but did not believe Conigliaro was ready for the big leagues. Pesky did—and that's all that mattered. Less than two years removed from high school ball, the 19-year-old was the starting center fielder for his hometown team.[2]

Conigliaro began with a bang, then a whimper. He homered in his first Fenway at-bat against White Sox standout right-hander Joel Horlen, then descended into a slump that lowered his batting mark to .152. But Conigliaro quickly rebounded and began to display the power and consistency that would mark his major-league career. His average remained over .270 from mid-June to season's end as he finished at .290 with 24 home runs in just 111 games. A broken arm ended Conigliaro's season prematurely and might have cost him Rookie of the Year honors. His .354 on-base percentage would prove to be his best.

The kid was the toast of the town. His status as an eligible bachelor was known around Boston and he even sang well enough to cut a local hit record appropriately titled "Playing the Field" that trumpeted a desire to remove the shackles of being a one-woman man in favor of freedom. He dated buxom blonde actress Mamie Van Doren, who was 14 years his senior. And when the Red Sox signed brother Billy, it seemed life could not get any better. Conigliaro led the league with 32 home runs in 1965, earning some votes in the Most Valuable Player balloting despite playing for a last-place team. He racked up 28 homers and a career-high 93 RBIs the following year at age 22 and seemed ready to rocket to superstardom. He was being compared to a young Mickey Mantle. Some began to talk about him potentially breaking Babe Ruth's all-time home-run record of 714.[3]

Nothing he did at the plate in 1967 changed that trajectory. Conigliaro was hitting better than ever as the Red Sox shockingly embarked on a pennant run. In July, he became the youngest player in baseball history to slug his 100th career home run. He had spent most of the season above .300, earning his first All-Star berth. But a troubling reality proved fateful. Conigliaro stood close to the plate and hung tough on inside fastballs. He was often hit by pitches. And players of that era did not wear ear flaps to protect their heads.

Angels part-time starter Jack Hamilton was not the ideal pitcher for any hitter who wished to stay healthy, especially one that crowded the dish. He was fast and wild. He worked to own the inside corner. He led the National League in walks as a rookie with the Phillies and never mastered the strike zone, finishing his career averaging about six walks per nine innings.

Fenway Park. August 18. Bottom of the fourth. Scoreless game. One on, one out. No balls, two strikes. Hamilton fires a 90-mph-plus fastball that gets away. Conigliaro is positioned so close to the plate that some claim the bill of his helmet is in the strike zone. He never moves. The ball lands so solidly just below the left temple that the thud can be heard around the park. An audible gasp, then silence. Conigliaro is bleeding from the ear, mouth, and nose. A horrified Hamilton rushes toward the plate but is stopped by catcher Buck Rodgers. "And I didn't want to look anymore," Rodgers said. "I told Jack, 'Get out of here, get away' . . . I pushed him back. I said, 'Jack, you don't want to see this.'"[4]

The iconic photo of Conigliaro's black eye did little justice to the severity of the damage. The blow, which Hamilton insists he never would have pitched intentionally, especially on an 0-2 count, broke Conigliaro's left cheekbone and dislocated his jaw. Conigliaro's life and career had changed in an awful instant. Nothing could ever be the same. "The roof fell in on me," he recalled. "My skull absorbed the full shock. Grabbing my head, I squeezed it hard, trying to stop the shriek that filled it, and at the same time I was gasping for breath. 'Oh God,' I prayed, 'Let me breathe. Let me live.'"[5]

Conigliaro lived. He died tragically young, but not before launching an inspiring and incredible comeback. He missed the rest of the 1967 and 1968 seasons with blurred vision. The lone bright spot for the Red Sox was that his absence allowed them to play Ken Harrelson in right

Mod outfielder Ken "Hawk" Harrelson before his 1969 trade to the lowly Indians.

field. "The Hawk" emerged as one of only two productive hitters on the team in The Year of the Pitcher in 1968 (the other being Yastrzemski) as he led the American League with 109 runs batted in. And the return of Conigliaro in 1969 provided an opportunity for the Sox to trade Harrelson to Cleveland for right-hander Sonny Siebert, who gave the team four strong seasons.

With one good eye, Conigliaro returned to the lineup in 1969 to hit 20 home runs. That was merely a precursor to a year in which it appeared he was all the way back. With brother Billy in the lineup as well in 1970, he set career highs with 36 home runs and 116 RBIs. The sky was again the limit.

That sky soon fell in on Conigliaro. He was dispatched to the Angels in a shocking trade during the offseason that many believe was precipitated by his conflicting relationship with Yastrzemski based on opposite personalities and motivations. Conigliaro was a bit of a playboy. Baseball came naturally to him. He was outgoing and good-looking. Yastrzemski was average-looking and introverted. He embraced the work ethic he believed necessary to thrive as a ballplayer. Baseball came easy to Conigliaro. The problem is that both were leaders. Some followed Yastrzemski. Others followed Conigliaro. And that split the team.

"There was a lot of dissension between Tony C. and Yaz," said pitcher Dennis Bennett. "You could see it in the clubhouse and in some ways on the field. They didn't talk to each other much. They didn't run around at all together. Tony had his group of friends, and Yaz had his. Yaz was a bit of a loner."[6]

General manager Dick O'Connell believed the presence of both Conigliaro brothers had a negative influence on the club. So he dealt Tony where he wanted to go if he indeed was banished from Boston— Southern California. Folks snickered when it was revealed he had taken a pad next door to ultimate sex symbol Raquel Welch.

He could certainly see the eye candy she had to offer, but he could not see fastballs and curves well enough anymore. His vision deteriorated. Conigliaro retired a half-season later after batting just .222 with the Angels. He made the Red Sox roster four years later in an aborted comeback but quit the sport for good after hitting a mere .123 in 21 games.

Life is not all about baseball and Conigliaro still had a bright future. He gained success as a sports anchor on the television news. But soon after New Year's Day in 1982, he suffered a heart attack that was followed by a stroke that placed him in a coma. When not hospitalized, he was forced to depend on Billy to take care of him. Conigliaro died at age 45 on February 24, 1990. But the memories of his talent lived on.

"If he hadn't been injured and had the eye problem, he was a definite Hall of Famer," said teammate Mike Andrews. "There was never a better clutch hitter than Tony."[7]

Chapter Twelve

A Great Pair of New Sox

That the Red Sox continued to rank among the premier offensive clubs in the sport in the early 1970s despite the loss of Conigliaro, dispatching George Scott to Milwaukee, and the inexplicable loss of power from Rico Petrocelli was a testament to many. General manager Dick O'Connell and his scouts continued to replenish the lineup with talent that included Hall of Fame catcher Carlton Fisk, speed demon Tommy Harper, brilliant all-around outfielder Dwight Evans, aging designated hitter Orlando Cepeda, and emerging first baseman Cecil Cooper. Carl Yastrzemski revitalized his career after two poor seasons that seemed to serve as a warning that age had caught up with him. And Reggie Smith maintained his production until a 1973 trade to St. Louis in a seemingly never-ending search for starting pitching.

Boston was not devoid of talented moundsmen. But O'Connell could not procure through the draft or trades until Roger Clemens rolled around in 1986, an ace that would prevent or halt losing streaks and lead the team through a pennant race. And no consistent, dependable starter emerged during that period. Sonny Siebert and Ray Culp pitched well in 1971, then faded. Marty Pattin did the same after peaking in 1972. Luis Tiant won 20 in 1973 but would never be the same as he hit his mid-30s. Bill Lee forged a fine career but was never an ace.

The Sox remained consistently strong. They won between 84 and 89 games every year from 1968 to 1974, but only in 1972 did they contend. They led the American League East heading into a three-game series against second-place Detroit and managed to score just two runs in the first two games to hand the crown to the Tigers. They were doomed by a late 7-19 swoon two years later.

The Red Sox had become perennial also-rans. The act was getting old. Somebody needed to breathe life into them. And two somebodies did. Their names were Fred Lynn and Jim Rice. Perhaps the greatest one-two rookie punch in baseball history could not have emerged from more disparate backgrounds. Lynn grew up in the Los Angeles suburbs, the son of an executive who had divorced his wife when the boy was 13. Rice was the product of segregated South Carolina. Integration finally forced him to unhappily leave his friends and attend a mostly white high school, but he endeared himself to the point he was voted co–class president.[12]

Soon their careers would follow similar paths. Both excelled in baseball and on the prep gridiron. Lynn declined an offer from the Yankees, who had selected him in the third round of the 1970 draft, to accept a football scholarship at the University of Southern California, then quickly turned to baseball. Rice could have taken a full ride to play wide receiver or defensive back at Clemson, North Carolina, or Nebraska. But he was chosen by the Red Sox in the first round in 1971 and decided to begin his professional baseball journey.

While Lynn was tearing up the college diamonds, slugging 21 home runs in just 310 at-bats while hitting .338 in two years with the Trojans, Rice was destroying minor-league pitching. He slammed 50 extra-base hits at Class A Winter Haven in 1972. The two met for the first time in 1973 at Double-A Bristol, where Rice proved based on his experience that his learning curve was ahead of Lynn's. While the latter struggled a bit getting his feet wet as a pro, Rice batted .317 with 27 home runs and 93 RBIs. The Red Sox understood Lynn's potential and promoted both to Triple-A Pawtucket a year later. They proved themselves as the lone bright lights on a dismal club. Rice was again better—he hit .337—but both were wearing Red Sox uniforms by the end of the year.

Lynn won a starting outfield job out of spring training in 1975 while Rice waited at designated hitter behind Tony Conigliaro, who was embarking on his ill-fated comeback. That rankled Rice, who had played longer and outperformed Lynn in the minors. He believed that race, not ability, was the primary consideration when the less experienced Lynn

Jim Rice finished second to Fred Lynn in the 1975 Rookie of the Year voting but forged a better career.

NATIONAL BASEBALL HALL OF FAME AND MUSEUM

was chosen to start over him. And three years later he raised the specter of racism in the Red Sox organization, causing a stir by revealing those thoughts in an interview with *Sport* magazine: "Race has to be a factor when Fred Lynn can hit .240 in the minors and I can hit .340 and he gets a starting job before I do," he said.[3]

Though Lynn managed a career .276 mark during his short stint in the minors, one can understand Rice's suspicions. Rice had not only hit far better before arriving in The Show, he had spent two more seasons than Lynn facing minor-league pitching. He did not apologize for his remarks after the *Sport* article was published, though he reaffirmed his commitment to the organization and respect for those that ran it.

Not that Rice remained out of the everyday lineup for long. The immense struggles of Conigliaro forced manager Darrell Johnson to insert the rookie into the full-time DH spot just one week into the regular season. Rice smashed two home runs in his first game in that role, slumped briefly in May, then spent the rest of the season raising his average, which remained permanently over .300 after a four-hit game at Yankee Stadium in late July.

Lynn also wasted no time justifying his quick ascension to the majors and inclusion in the lineup. He took the Sox and the sport by storm, batting .556 with three home runs during an eight-game hitting streak in April and just continued to rake. Lynn never slumped as he kept his average above .300 from that point forward, peaking at .361 in early June. His five-hit, three-homer game that month against Detroit remains one of the most prolific hitting exhibitions in baseball history.

The baseball world was mesmerized by the two rookies, who were known as the Gold Dust Twins for reasons that remain unknown (the original Gold Dust Twins were created as the trademark for a product called Fairbank's Gold Dust Washing Powder in 1892). They were also captivated by the team for which they played. Fueled by Lynn and Rice, as well as catcher Carlton Fisk when he returned from a devastating thumb injury, the Red Sox overcame poor seasons from Yastrzemski and the fading Petrocelli to rank first in the American League in runs scored. They leaped into the pennant race from the start, took control of the Eastern Division with a 10-game winning streak in July, then hung on for the crown. The feat was quite remarkable considering that Boston finished ninth in the league in team ERA and dead last in home runs allowed, despite credible performances by starters Bill Lee, Luis Tiant, Rick Wise, and Roger Moret, whose insertion into the rotation sparked the Sox.

Among those impressed by the new Sox was old Sox star Hawk Harrelson, who had launched his career as a baseball analyst by working their TV broadcasts. Harrelson not only cited the offensive impact of Rice and Lynn, but the team defense that included the former when he took over in left field, as well as the brilliant Dwight Evans. "How many times do you get two guys (Rice and Lynn) coming in like that?" he asked. "Maybe every 50 years, every 100 years . . . I knew we would score runs. But nothing hit the ground in the outfield. The outfield defense was spectacular."[4]

The offense, defense, and opportunity to win the World Series for the first time in 57 years took a hit when Rice sustained a season-ending injury, breaking his hand on a pitch by Detroit right-hander Vern Ruhle on September 21. The figurative and literal bad break with just five days left in the regular season forced others to step up offensively in the American League Championship Series—and they did. Among them was emerging star slugger Cecil Cooper, who batted .400 in a three-game sweep of defending World Series champion Oakland. Yastrzemski, who had been greatly unproductive in the regular season due to age, a shoulder injury, and emotional hardship caused by a dying mother, rose to the occasion by batting .455. And while Lynn and Fisk were doing their usual damage, a pitching staff that ranked ninth in the AL in team ERA performed brilliantly. The fiercely competitive Tiant allowed just one unearned run in a complete-game victory to open the series, reliever Dick Drago blanked the Athletics over three innings to save Game 2, and Rick Wise shut them down into the eighth to clinch a spot in the Fall Classic.

And what a classic it was. The 1975 World Series is considered by many the greatest ever played. The rollercoaster ride never stopped. Heroes emerged on both sides as the Sox battled Cincinnati, the only team in baseball that season that outscored them. The Big Red Machine boasted three Hall of Famers—and another that should have been, had

Hall of Fame catcher Carlton Fisk, whose legendary home run won Game 6 of the 1975 World Series.
NATIONAL BASEBALL HALL OF FAME AND MUSEUM

he not gambled on baseball—in catcher Johnny Bench, first baseman Tony Pérez, second baseman Joe Morgan, and third baseman Pete Rose. Some feel left fielder George Foster and shortstop Dave Concepción merit inclusion as well. And, unlike the Red Sox, the Reds even finished near the top of their league in team ERA. It is no wonder they finished with a record of 108-54 and won the most games by a National League team since Pittsburgh snagged 110 in 1909 and matched since only by the 1986 Mets.

Johnson picked Tiant to start Game 1. The Cuban right-hander affectionately nicknamed El Tiante experienced a career filled with performance peaks and valleys, but he was certainly peaking down the stretch in 1975. He'd pitched three complete games that included two shutouts in his last four starts of the regular season before stifling the Athletics in the ALCS. It was hoped that the variety of unorthodox windups and deliveries in which he often turned his back to home plate would throw off the timing of the Cincinnati sluggers, though they did not strike out often. Tiant rode a six-run seventh inning that he launched with a single to a five-hit shutout.

Rose wasn't fazed by the windup and delivery, offering that he just looked for the ball anyway. But he was certainly thrown off by the pitch selection in going 0-for-4. "Our reports told us that 80 percent of his pitches were fastballs," he complained. "We even saw films of him blowing them past [Oakland hitters Sal Bando and Reggie Jackson]. So that's what we were looking for. I couldn't believe what we saw. We haven't got anybody in the National League like that, nobody who throws spinning high curveballs that take two minutes to come down!"[5]

Wise seemed likely to be tabbed for the Game 2 start, but coach and soon-to-be-manager Don Zimmer put a bug in Johnson's ear, suggesting that crafty southpaw Bill Lee was better suited to thwart the Cincinnati bats with his offspeed stuff. Johnson took the advice and ran with it. Lee performed brilliantly, taking a 2–1 lead into the ninth, but was removed when Bench led off with a double. Drago retired the first two he faced. The Sox were one out from a 2–0 series lead. He induced Concepción to chop one into the ground, but it bounced through the middle for a single that tied it. Then Ken Griffey, whose fine career will forever be overshadowed by that of his namesake son, slammed a double that ultimately sent the Sox to defeat.

Boston turned the tables in Game 3 with a ninth-inning rally of its own. A two-run homer by Evans over the Green Monster knotted the score at 5–5. Soon one of the most controversial plays in the history of the sport would add fuel to the fire of those who believed in the Curse of the Bambino. After Cesar Geronimo singled to start the Cincinnati 10th, career bench warmer Ed Armbrister bounced a bunt barely in front of home plate. He hesitated before taking off to first as he and Fisk collided. The catcher snagged the ball and fired it wildly to second in a vain attempt to force Geronimo, allowing both runners to move up a base. Home plate umpire Larry Barnett did not call Armbrister out for interference. Johnson shot out of the dugout to argue. Barnett refused to confer with another umpire and the call stood. Soon Morgan was winning the game with an RBI single.

A furious Fisk, who got tangled with Armbrister reaching the ball but was unimpeded throwing it to second, confronted Barnett (who was soon receiving death threats from unreasonably incensed Red Sox fans) after all hell broke loose. Fisk remained convinced that Armbrister had initially interfered. "Armbrister came up under me as I was going for the ball," Fisk said. "I felt like I was hit by a linebacker . . . It's a damn shame to lose a ball game like that. One call from an umpire can change the complexion of the whole Series. If I don't think I've got a legitimate complaint, I'm not the kind who will beef and moan and make a show."[6]

One can only speculate if Tiant was fazed early in Game 4 by the bizarre and sad ending the previous night, but he allowed two runs in the first and two more in the fourth before locking in. He pitched in and out of jams the rest of the way, requiring only a five-run explosion by his teammates in the fourth to tie the series at 2–2. But the Red Sox were on the eve of destruction after Pérez slammed two home runs in Game 5 to power Cincinnati to victory.

The winner the next three nights was Mother Nature. Downpours pushed back Game 6. Then baseball commissioner Bowie Kuhn chickened out after originally scheduling the nationally televised game on October 20, which would challenge the sport to a Nielsen rating battle against Monday Night Football and the popular sitcom *All in the Family*. The mini-vacation finally ended when the teams returned to Fenway on Tuesday night for perhaps the most memorable and electrifying baseball game ever played.

The delay allowed Johnson to tab Tiant to save the season. After Lynn launched a three-run homer in the first and Tiant tossed four shutout innings, destiny seemed to be pointing to a Game 7. But Tiant collapsed, allowing six runs over the next four innings while a succession of Reds relievers shut down the Sox, who appeared doomed heading into the bottom of the eighth. That's when Cincinnati closer Rawly Eastwick, who had led the National League in saves, arrived with two on and two out. Pinch-hitter Bernie Carbo, a former Red and forgotten man after he had lost his starting job to Evans, sent a high fastball soaring over the center field wall to tie it. And Rose, after the ball disappeared into the crowd, displayed a sense of appreciation for the dramatics rather than anger at the turn of events. "Win or lose, Popeye," he told third base coach Don Zimmer, "we're in the greatest game ever played."[7]

Carbo's home run was among the biggest blasts in baseball history. Yet it wasn't even the biggest blast of the game. That distinction would be reserved for the 12th exhausting inning, after Drago and Wise had ground the Big Red Machine to a halt. It was 12:34 a.m. Reds reliever Pat Darcy on the mound. Fisk at the plate. Darcy was a low-ball pitcher. Fisk was a low-ball hitter. Darcy tossed one high. Ball one. Then he fired a fastball at the knees that caught a bit too much of the plate and way too much of the bat. Fisk mashed it deep down the left field line. That it had the distance was certain. That it would stay fair was not. In a moment that would remain indelibly etched in the memories of baseball fans throughout the world, Fisk hopped out of the box and with a sharp movement of his arms tried to will the ball fair. Mission accomplished. Game over. One more night of baseball.

It was almost a shame there had to be. "Call it off. Call the seventh game off. Let the World Series stand this way, three games for the Cincinnati Reds and three for the Boston Red Sox," wrote *Boston Globe* sports columnist Ray Fitzgerald, only half-joking.[8]

The historical greatness of Game 6 obscures that of a fine finale that pitted Reds ace Don Gullett against Lee, who Johnson wished he had started the night before.[9] The Sox took their momentum and ran with it, though Gullett's wildness certainly helped. He walked four in the third inning (including Fisk intentionally). The last two with the bases loaded scored runs, but Boston proved unable to add to its 3–0 lead while Lee was mowing down some of the best hitters in baseball. The Red Sox had already wasted a leadoff double in the second. They had a runner on third with one out in the fourth and failed to score. They loaded the bases in the fifth—no dice.

Soon Lee was learning a lesson. He had been warned before the game to save his "Leephus" pitch—an offshoot of the high-arching "eephus" pitch made famous in the 1960s by Yankees pitcher Steve Hamilton—when facing Pérez. Scouting reports indicated that Pérez murdered slow curves. But here it came in the sixth with one on and two out. The Cincinnati slugger rocketed a tape-measure blast over the Green Monster and onto Lansdowne Street to close the gap to 3–2. Lee later used his wry sense of humor to explain what happened.

"I had been having good success with Tony, throwing him my slow, arching curveball, so I thought it would be a good idea to throw it to him again," Lee explained. "Unfortunately, so did Tony, who timed it beautifully. He counted the seams of the ball as it floated up to the plate, checked to see if [American League president] Lee MacPhail's signature was on it, signed his own name to it, and then jumped all over it. He hit the ball over the left-field screen and several small buildings."[10]

The Reds had wrested the momentum away and would never give it up. A finger blister forced Lee out in the seventh. He was replaced by Moret, who didn't have it. He gave up an RBI single to Rose sandwiched between two walks. The lead had evaporated. The game remained tied into the ninth, when Johnson summoned rookie left-hander Jim Burton, who had performed well down the stretch before fading into obscurity. Burton allowed two more walks before Morgan dumped a weakly hit single into center for the go-ahead run as screeching Boston fans fell silent. Soon the Reds were enjoying a raucous celebration and the Red Sox title drought had reached 57 years.

All that remained were nagging thoughts about what could have been. Would the Sox have won the series had Rice played? What if Lee had kept that blooper pitch in his mind and not on the mound? Why did Johnson use a rookie pitcher with the score tied in the ninth inning of Game 7? None of it really mattered. One cannot turn back the hands of time. And 29 more years would pass before all the frustration would melt away in the afterglow of a championship.

Chapter Thirteen

The So-Called Spaceman

THE ABILITY AND DESIRE TO CONFORM HAVE GENERALLY AND FOREVER
been considered positive attributes for athletes in team sports. Every
baseball season is like a new journey that sets sail in February and ends in
October. And one should not rock the boat. Never mind the in-fighting
that plagued the Oakland Athletics and New York Yankees of the 1970s.
Never mind that they won World Series titles. They were anomalies,
exceptions to the rule.

So was Bill Lee, who gave credence to what was generally believed
to be a silly notion that left-handers are flakes. Lee bristled at his
"Spaceman" nickname, preferring that others perceived him as smart,
honest, outspoken, and fiercely competitive. He tolerated no less effort
and sensibility on the field of play than he did from himself. His criti-
cisms of teammates and even managers were endured, though not always
accepted, by the Red Sox during his heyday from 1971 to 1975 because
he boasted a 67-41 record during that stretch with an earned run average
under 4.00 in each of those seasons as one of baseball's best junkballers.

That Lee played with passion is undeniable. But calling him offbeat
off the field is equally irrefutable, especially in an era in which baseball
players shied away from social and political issues. He was a candid pac-
ifist and antiwar activist during the tail end of American involvement in
Vietnam. He was an outspoken environmentalist. He railed against the
effects of greed on the capitalist system, as well as criticism of a judge
that ordered busing to combat school desegregation in Boston. He spoke
about the need to decriminalize marijuana, which he admitted to sprin-

kling on his buckwheat pancakes and thus earned a fine from baseball commissioner Bowie Kuhn.

Lee was a product of his upbringing both in Southern California and San Francisco, as well as his USC education and desire to become more learned in pursuits outside baseball. Unlike most kids growing up in the 1950s and early 1960s, he had no heroes. He embraced playing the sport but not those who excelled in it professionally. Not that he always played it correctly as a child. His interpretation of the rules helped him realize that he was not quite like other kids. So did other odd manifestations of his thinking and behavior.

"My parents made the big mistake when they put me in school too early," he said. "Four years old, I handcuffed myself to the bedpost. Screwed myself forever. . . . In our kickball game during recess from Holy Communion class I booted the ball and ran the bases third to second to first. A triple the wrong way. From that moment I was a goner."[1]

Whether or not Lee knew the right direction back to home plate, he continued to happily break rules he deemed archaic or unnecessary. He performed well enough academically to land a scholarship to USC, though he later claimed he would have preferred majoring in forestry at Humboldt State or attending UCLA, which churned out more radical students during the turbulent 1960s. Though Lee hated the elitism he perceived as permeating the USC campus, he remained there for four years and, in quintessential Lee fashion, earned a degree in geography.

Lee wanted to hit and pitch at USC and even boycotted preseason practice one year unless coach Rod Dedeaux agreed to let him play some first base. He returned when he was given the green light to take batting practice. But it was on the mound where he thrived, developing a huge assortment of offspeed pitches and compiling a career record of 38-8 that included a pair of victories in the 1968 College World Series. Despite a distinct lack of velocity, he challenged hitters enough with his fastball to keep them off-balance and put them away with his breaking pitches.

A lack of heat on the heater, partially due to a knee injury in high school that prevented him from pushing off the mound, resulted in Lee waiting until the 22nd round of the 1968 draft to be selected by the Sox and get sent to Class A Waterloo. Lee befuddled batters at that level with his sinker and fadeaway, striking out nearly a batter an inning that season. His talent resulted in a rare promotion from that level to the big leagues the following year. But Fisk, who was also rising through the Boston farm system at the time, recalled more about Lee than his pitching. And it was quite the eye-opener given his rural New Hampshire background.

"The prevailing atmosphere in Iowa was a whole lot of screaming matches between Bill and the manager," Fisk remembered. "There was no way Bill would have anything to do with discipline or authority. He was way ahead of all of us, both in age and worldliness, and he resented being treated like a teenager, which most of the players were. I had never met anybody from California before. It was wild. His cares and priorities and morals were at the opposite end of the rainbow from mine. . . . He was always questioning the manager. Why, why, why?"[2]

What the Red Sox asked about Lee in 1969 was "Why not?" They promoted him after a brilliant stint at Double-A Pittsfield. He lost most of 1970 as the last Red Sox player to be tabbed for a stint in the Army Reserve, then returned in 1971 to serve as a long reliever behind a veteran, but bad, rotation. Lee was lucky to have pitched when his teammates were scoring, as his 9-2 record despite a poor 1.452 WHIP attests. He performed better out of the bullpen in 1972, then blossomed as a starter. His fine control, penchant for pitching out of jams, and run support from a typically deadly Sox offense resulted in a 17-11 record and career-best (as a starter) 2.75 ERA in 1973.

Lee emerged as a rotation mainstay, winning 17 games in three consecutive seasons. Though he slumped in 1976 after he injured his shoulder in a brawl with the Yankees, he rebounded to perform well the next two years before a trade to Montreal after the 1978 season, during which he had called Red Sox general manager Haywood Sullivan, who was also part-owner since the death of Tom Yawkey in 1976, "gutless" and criticized manager Don Zimmer. He then bolted the team for 24 hours after best friend and 1975 World Series hero Bernie Carbo was sold to Cleveland. Zimmer bypassed him for a critical start against the Yankees in the heat of the pennant race in favor of rookie Bobby Sprowl, who was creamed in a 7–4 defeat. Given that the Red Sox finished the

Flaky lefty Bill Lee enjoyed some great years before growing disenchanted with Sox management.

NATIONAL BASEBALL HALL OF FAME AND MUSEUM

regular season tied for first with the Bronx Bombers and lost the pennant in a playoff, that decision arguably cost Boston a shot at a World Series title. But one could argue that Zimmer based his move on performance rather than emotion. Lee had lost seven consecutive starts to lower his record to 10-10 heading into the stretch run.[3]

Don Zimmer managed the Sox to some fine seasons but could not break the Curse.
NATIONAL BASEBALL HALL OF FAME AND MUSEUM

Lee's struggles on the mound could be traced back to the dispatching of Carbo to the Indians. Though he won his next four decisions, he pitched well only twice before collapsing. Lee and Carbo were infuriated that the Red Sox got nobody in return for the latter, who was swapped for half the waiver price. Lee left the club to join Carbo for dinner and plenty of booze that night. Carbo urged Lee to return to the ballpark but to no avail. And when Lee did confront Sullivan the next day, all hell broke loose. Lee believed the GM had dumped Carbo for virtually nothing because he was a free spirit who wanted little more out of life than to enjoy it and hit pinch-hit home runs.

"Haywood started yelling and ranting and raving at me," Lee recalled years later. "'Why did you do this? Do that?' I said, 'You can't do this to the ballclub. You sold Bernie for half the waiver price. You did it to punish him.'" Lee accused him of other examples of mistreatment of Carbo, to which Sullivan replied that it was none of his business and proceeded to fine the lefty $500 for going AWOL. Lee responded that he should be fined $1,500 so he could take the whole weekend off. Soon Lee was confronting Zimmer as well, calling him a horse's ass and lying cocksucker.[4]

The losing streak was the last straw. Despite performing well in three early September relief appearances, Lee did not pitch again for the Red Sox, even over the last three weeks of one of the most intense pennant races in baseball history. Zimmer, who had yearned to release the lefty in July before the front office interceded, told Lee that the team did not need him. And one can argue that, at least in that case, he was right. Boston won 12 of 14 without him to take a one-game lead before faltering.

Lee rebounded for one last hurrah with the Expos in 1979 before his career petered out. All Red Sox fans had memories of the quirky southpaw. But they were memories that could bring smiles to faces for generations to come. Like the time he wore a Daniel Boone mask on the field. Or the time he donned a beanie with a propeller between the lines. Or the time he took a spontaneous trip to China, then grew a beard he named the "Ho Chi Minh." Or the time he described pitching as a form of sexual expression. Or the time he told the media that Zimmer "wouldn't know a good pitcher if he came up and bit him in the ass."[5]

Time often brings clarity. And the baseball world will remember Bill Lee for both his faults and his attributes. But most of all, he will be remembered for bringing badly needed personality into a sport that has grown more lacking of it since he retired.

Chapter Fourteen

Bucky Freaking Dent and the Pain of '78

TIME CAN ON OCCASION MUDDLE MEMORY. RED SOX FANS WHO LIVED through the journey in 1978 recall most vividly how it ended. They cringe at the thought of a late slump that wiped out a big lead and a weak-hitting Yankee shortstop blasting one over the Green Monster to extend the Curse of the Bambino another year.

But details abound about the era and specific season that are not so readily remembered. Among them is that the Sox also experienced a painful collapse in 1977 that cost them a potential pennant. They rebounded from a mediocre 25-23 start with a 16-2 run, then overcame a nine-game losing streak launched by a three-game sweep at Yankee Stadium to win 29 of their next 39. Included was a 16-1 tear that catapulted them 3½ games atop the Eastern Division with late August approaching. But while New York began to build on its 40-10 run in August and September, the Sox lost seven in a row to lose the team's grip on the lead. They got scorching hot to finish the year, but the Yankees never cooled off. They won five straight with the season winding down yet could not gain a game on the Bronx Bombers, who went on to capture their first World Series crown since 1962.

One cannot claim a campaign in which the Sox won 97 games was a waste. But they did not take full advantage of career or last productive years from several players. Included among them was Yastrzemski, whose .296 batting average, 28 home runs, and 102 RBIs were numbers that he would never again match. The season marked the last hurrah for veteran first baseman George Scott, who at age 33 bashed 33 home runs. He would not hit more than 12 thereafter. Catcher Carlton Fisk enjoyed his best all-around performance, batting .315 with 102 RBIs. Second-year third baseman Butch Hobson would not repeat his 30-home-run, 112-RBI production in a career that simply petered out before he hit 30. Shortstop Rick Burleson managed arguably his finest effort in 1977. So did closer Bill "Soup" Campbell, who recorded a career-best 31 saves and earned his only All-Star appearance.

Another vaguer recollection is that seeds of discontent had been planted long before the end of that season. Dissatisfaction rooted in a generation gap festered as relationships between players and old-school manager Don Zimmer deteriorated. It was especially prevalent among pitchers and iconoclasts such as Carbo, who in 1977, along with hurlers Ferguson Jenkins, Jim Willoughby, Bill Lee, and Rick Wise formed what famously became known as the Buffalo Head Gang. Jenkins founded the band of Boston rebels in their disrespect of Zimmer, whom they deemed looked like a buffalo, which they contended was an ugly and stupid animal. Their anti-Zimmer sentiments were not merely based on the conservatism that left him behind the times but also on what they perceived as his poor management of the staff. They believed his five-man rotations, which had yet to be embraced by most baseball managers, threw off their timing and preparation.

Zimmer and general manager Dick O'Connell spent much of 1978 getting rid of the malcontents. Jenkins, Willoughby, and Wise were dispatched before spring training, then Carbo and Lee were gone before the calendar turned to 1979. "Zimmer thought we were a danger to his ballclub," Lee explained. "He was of the old school, and we were part of the counter-culture. He and the front office thought that we were going to corrupt the morals of the rest of the team."[1]

What is also overshadowed by the epic playoff defeat in 1978 is that the Red Sox did not choke so much as the Yankees rose to the occasion. The Boston lead over New York peaked at 14 games on July 19, but its first-place advantage was just nine games over upstart Milwaukee. The Sox owned an unsustainable .689 winning percentage. A slump seemed inevitable, and the Red Sox experienced two. A 2-10 slide in late July allowed the Brewers to chop their deficit to 4½ games before they faded. The Sox recovered to win 21 of 31 to hold off the sizzling Yankees. The grip on first place remained at seven games on August 30. Then came the doozy of slumps, a 3-13 disaster that included six losses to New York and sent the Sox out of sole possession of the lead for the rest of the year. But it should be remembered that the Red Sox finished the regular season with a 12-2 stretch that forced the legendary playoff.

The rollercoaster ride of 1978 began with promise, the result not only of an established, talent-laden lineup but also the additions of free agent starter Mike Torrez, whom they signed away from the hated Yankees, and of super side-arming starting right-hander and future Hall of Famer Dennis Eckersley, for whom the Red Sox fleeced Cleveland in exchange for an aging Wise, as well as highly touted third base prospect and major-league flop Ted Cox. Eckersley, Torrez, and emerging Bob Stanley, who won 15 games mostly as a reliever to offset the collapse of Campbell, headed a pitching staff that finished a heady fourth in the American League in team earned run average.

Those hurlers allowed Boston to dominate after a slow start to the season. When they got hot, so did the Red Sox. During a torrid 45-15 run that lasted from May 3 to July 8, the staff held opponents to four runs or less in 46 of 60 games, including 12 straight to start the tear. Opponents managed to score just 13 runs during a five-game Sox winning streak in mid-July that included a four-game sweep of Minnesota. They appeared destined to run away and hide in the American League East.

But in quite untraditional Red Sox fashion, it was the bats that fell silent as the team began its slide into ignominious history. During a six-game stretch that concluded the 2-10 slump, they scored five total runs. The offense righted itself, but bad luck and bad pitching took its toll. Shoulder and back problems plagued Yastrzemski. Fisk cracked a rib. Hobson suffered from cartilage damage in both knees and bone chips in his elbow. Campbell pitched all season with a shoulder injury. The physical issues caught up with the Red Sox, who had lost their momentum and all but four games off their lead over the Yankees when they welcomed that team to Fenway Park for a critical four-game series starting on September 7. The Boston Massacre was about to begin.

Sidearmer Dennis Eckersley won 20 for the Sox in 1978 before Oakland converted him into a closer.

The first victim was Torrez, whose inconsistencies had descended into a full-blown slump in August. An error by Hobson, whose injuries had badly affected his fielding, led to a two-run first inning, then Torrez allowed four straight singles to open the second and motivate Zimmer to give him the hook. Soon it was 12–0. Game over.

Second-game starter Jim Wright managed to retire only one more batter than Torrez. He too was bombed out in the second inning, after which New York boasted an 8–0 lead. So desperate was Zimmer to prevent his bullpen from overwork that he called upon Lee, the pitcher he despised, to complete the lost cause. Most disturbing was the Red Sox committed a whopping seven errors, showing a numbing tightness or a distinct lack of focus—or both.

One might have figured the ultra-confident Eckersley would step up the next day in a nationally televised showdown—and he did for three innings. Four hits, three walks, one error, and a passed ball later, the Yankees led 7–0. And there it would stay as super lefty Ron Guidry pitched a two-hitter as his team pulled to within one game of the lead. And when Zimmer ignored Lee to start rookie Bobby Sprowl the next afternoon, it seemed a foregone conclusion that the battle for the top of the American League would be knotted. It was indeed, as Sprowl never made it out of the first inning.

Red Sox starting pitching surrendered 14 earned runs in 6⅔ innings during the four-game series. They were outscored 42–9. They committed 12 errors. Two more defeats at Yankee Stadium a week later made it 13 of 16. But it was the Boston Massacre that would earn an infamous place in Red Sox history.

"How could a team get 30-something games over .500 in July and then in September see its pitching, hitting and fielding all fall apart at the same time?" Fisk wondered after the series. Added Yastrzemski optimistically as he stared into his locker, "It's never easy to win a pennant. We've got three weeks to play. . . . Anything can happen."[2]

Indeed. And what did happen would have been rejected as too implausible for a Hollywood script and as cruel and unusual punishment for Red Sox Nation. A do-or-die defeat of the host Yankees ended the 3-13 slide, inched Boston to within 2½ games of first place, and launched the 12-2 tear. Tiant kept the Sox alive with a brilliant two-hit shutout of visiting Toronto on the final day of the regular season, forcing a playoff as Indians starter Rick Waits pitched eight shutout innings after a two-run first to beat New York. The Fenway crowd learned of that happy news when the scoreboard flashed the score and a bit of appreciation: "CLV 9 NY 2 Thank you Rick Waits." That a southpaw shackled the Yankees gave fuel to the fire of the lefty Lee, whose strong performances in relief during the Boston Massacre left many wondering why he did not start over Sprowl.[3]

That was water under the bridge on the warm afternoon of Monday, October 2, the day of the Yankee invasion. Fenway was packed for the first American League playoff since the Red Sox lost the 1948 pennant to the Indians at the same venue. The pitching matchup favored New York, which had brilliant lefty Ron Guidry rested and on his usual roll. He had all but completed one of the greatest seasons in baseball history, arriving with a 24-3 record, 1.72 ERA, and one earned run allowed over 18 innings in his previous two starts. He had twice blanked Boston in September. The Red Sox countered with the inconsistent Torrez, who had somehow shut out Detroit in his last outing despite allowing seven walks.

Torrez outpitched the Cy Young Award winner through six. Guidry had neither his usual velocity nor sharp movement. The 39-year-old Yastrzemski added to his Hall of Fame credentials by launching a home run in the second inning, then Rice singled in another run in the sixth. In a display of arrogance and counting the old chickens before they're hatched, Red Sox fans began chanting "The Yankees suck, the Yankees suck."

Meanwhile, Torrez was shooting down the Bronx Bombers inning after inning. He had hurled a two-hitter heading to the seventh. By that time the wind had shifted. It was blowing out toward left. Lee later claimed to have predicted such an occurrence that morning. And by that time he felt he should have been brought into the game to relieve Torrez. But the starter appeared likely to escape a jam that inning when light-hitting Bucky Dent strode to the plate with two on and two out. The Yankees could only hope that their ninth hitter would somehow find a way to get on base to bring up the far more dangerous Mickey Rivers.

One wondered why Yankees manager Bob Lemon didn't pinch-hit for Dent. It proved equally questionable if the .240-hitting shortstop would even remain in the game after fouling a ball off his foot and taking treatment from trainers for several minutes. But he returned to the batter's box with a 1-1 count. Then Torrez threw a meatball over the heart of the plate that Dent sent soaring down the left field line. Perceiving a long out, Torrez began walking off the mound as Yastrzemski pounded his glove in anticipation. But the strong wind had taken hold of the ball and dropped it into the net atop the Green Monster for Dent's first home run in six weeks. Yankees 3, Red Sox 2.

"I lost some of my concentration during the delay," Torrez said. "It was about four minutes, but it felt like an hour. I had thought they'd pinch-hit for Dent with maybe Jay Johnstone or Cliff Johnson. I felt good. I just wanted to get going. . . . During the delay, I thought slider on the next pitch. But Fisk and me were working so well together, I went along with his call for a fastball. When Dent hit it, I thought we were out of the inning."[4]

The Red Sox had not blown it yet, but Torrez was clearly shaken. He departed after walking Rivers, then Stanley allowed another run to score on a Thurman Munson double off the Monster that stretched the Boston deficit to 4–2. A Reggie Jackson homer in the eighth made it 5–2. The Sox appeared doomed, but they came to life in the eighth against overpowering Yankees closer Goose Gossage. A Jerry Remy leadoff double and singles by Yastrzemski, Fisk, and Lynn closed the gap to 5–4. But Gossage retired Hobson and Scott to end the inning.

The Sox continued to battle back against Gossage in the ninth. The fervent hopes of Sox fans everywhere rose when a Burleson walk and Remy single placed runners on first and second with Rice and Yastrzemski due up. The outcome of the game might have been different had Burleson tried for third on the single, but he believed it to be too risky. He would then have scored when Rice launched a long flyball that was caught near the warning track.

A battle for the ages was set. Gossage vs. Yastrzemski. The young flamethrower had led the league in saves and fanned nearly a batter an inning, a mean feat in those days. The grizzled veteran had risen to the occasion time and again in the clutch. "I thought: Freeze this minute," Red Sox fan and author Jonathan Schwartz wrote in a 1979 essay about his feelings at that moment. "I gazed down at [Yastrzemski] through tears. I thought: 'Freeze it right here. How unspeakably beautiful it is. Everyone, reach out and touch it.'"[5]

Soon Gossage was firing a 1-0 fastball, low and in. Yastrzemski tried to pull it through the hole, but the ball arrived quicker than expected. He popped it up the opposite way. Sure-handed Yankee third baseman Graig Nettles drifted back and snagged it. Game over. Season over. The anger and frustration caused by blowing a 14-game lead sunk in permanently for the Red Sox and their fans. The "what ifs" proved emotionally overwhelming.

And when it was over, one and all could remember the words Yastrzemski uttered before the showdown. "After all that has happened to both teams this is probably the only way this should be settled," he said. "But I feel sorry that either team must lose. The two best teams in baseball, the greatest rivalry in sports. There should be no loser. I know that after the way this team came back, I'll always think of it as one thing—the winner."[6]

Yastrzemski certainly could not have convinced Red Sox fans of that as they shuffled out of Fenway, some in tears, around 5:30 p.m. on October 2, 1978.

CHAPTER FIFTEEN

Rocket Roger

IT WAS JUNE 6, 1983. TEAM SCOUTS AND GENERAL MANAGERS HAD prepared all year for that day. It was time for the Major League Baseball draft.

The annual crapshoot tests ability to forecast player success. Advanced metrics in recent years have brought more scientific analysis into the process. But back then the eye test, basic statistical research, and a study of character and make-up were the only measuring sticks.

Right-handed pitchers quickly came off the board. The Twins wasted their top overall pick on Tim Belcher, who refused to sign with them, opting instead to compete at the college level. Other hurlers were taken. Stan Hilton. Jackie Davidson. Darrel Akerfelds. Ray Hayward. Joel Davis. Rich Stoll. Wayne Dotson. Brian Holman. Eric Sonberg. Names that would soon be swept into the dustbin of history.

The Red Sox owned the 19th selection. And they plucked a right-hander named Roger Clemens from the University of Texas. Little could anyone have imagined the impact he would have on the team, the city, and the sport. While nearly all of those chosen ahead of him would never grace a major-league mound while the others aside from Belcher enjoyed little more than a cup of coffee at that level, Clemens would blossom into one of the greatest and most controversial pitchers in baseball history.

Clemens lost two fathers in his youth—one whom he claimed to have spoken with just once after a split with his mom when the child was merely five months old and the other eight years later to an early death. But the young Clemens did not lose direction in life as he turned instead to older brother Randy, whose athletic prowess in high school inspired him. Roger adopted the philosophy of his sibling—either you're a winner or you're a failure. A substance abuse problem played a role in preventing Randy from maximizing his athletic talents, but his younger brother remained on the straight and narrow until his competitive nature got the best of him during his major-league career.

In high school he had yet to develop the blazing fastball that defined his greatness, but he did land a scholarship at San Jacinto Junior College, where coach Wayne Graham encouraged him to become more explosive in his delivery. Soon Clemens had established himself as the ace of the staff, which motivated the Mets to select him in the 12th round of the 1981 draft. He instead followed his heart to the University of Texas, his dream school, where he competed against the best in college baseball and blossomed into a premier major-league prospect. He finished his two seasons there with a 25-7 record, 2.62 ERA, and nearly a strikeout per inning.[1]

Only mechanical issues prevented Clemens from being selected higher in 1983. Wrote Chicago White Sox scout Larry Monroe: "Delivery is fluid but does not use body at all. Should be easily improved and no reason why he shouldn't be in the low 90s. I'm surprised he doesn't have shoulder problems from standing up and just throwing. Some bend in legs and drive to plate would help velocity, life and location."[2]

Another scout was equally skeptical, offering the following in his appraisal of Clemens: "Good strong pitcher's body. Has a good arm. Fastball has [average velocity]. Most of the game was 87-90 [miles per hour]. Curve had [good] rotation. Slider was sharp early in game. Control was only fair. Didn't see a straight change. Fastball doesn't have much movement when in strike zone."[3]

Both scouting reports indicated a long and arduous trek to the big leagues for Clemens. But the right-hander skyrocketed through the Boston organization in one of the most dominant runs of minor-league pitching in franchise history. Peaking at Double-A in 1983, he won seven of nine decisions with a WHIP of 0.802, allowed just two home runs in 81 innings, walked 12, and fanned 95. He made four starts at Triple-A Pawtucket to open the following season, but the pitching-poor Red Sox

Volatile right-hander Roger Clemens flashes the form that made him one of the best pitchers in the American League.
WIKIMEDIA COMMONS

couldn't wait much longer. They promoted the 21-year-old for a mid-May start against Cleveland.

Clemens proved far from overpowering his rookie season. He compiled a fine 9-4 record but struggled for the first time in his career with a 4.32 earned run average and more hits allowed than innings pitched. The following year brought greater doubt and misery. He lowered his ERA to 3.29 but nagging injuries limited him to just 15 starts. He hit rock bottom on July 7 in Anaheim when sharp shoulder pain prevented him from making his start against the Angels. He broke down tearfully in the clubhouse as he questioned his baseball mortality before being placed on the disabled list with inflammation. He returned for two strong starts in August, but the pain persisted. Soon he was going under the knife as famed surgeon James Andrews removed a small piece of cartilage from the damaged area. The antsy right-hander could do nothing but rehab and wait for the 1986 season to prove himself healthy and productive.

That he would blossom into arguably the greatest pitcher in franchise history and certainly the finest since Cy Young could not be predicted. But he certainly arrived at an opportune time. The Sox had fallen from perennial pennant contender to also-ran in the years preceding his debut, mostly due to a weak rotation. An aging Mike Torrez had faltered. Dennis Eckersley had fallen victim to alcoholism and descended into mediocrity until his conversion to the closer role in Oakland transformed him into a Hall of Famer. Boston pitching ranked either 9th or 11th in American League team ERA every season from 1980 to 1983. The Sox finished under .500 in the last of those years for the first time since 1966. Lynn had been shipped to the Angels in a terrible trade that brought vastly talented left-hander Frank Tanana, who could not fulfill his promise, and veteran outfielder Joe Rudi, who was cooked.

The launching of the Clemens era proved coincidentally the end of the Yastrzemski era. The second-last game of the miserable 1983 season brought joy to a sellout crowd at Fenway as Yaz Day celebrated his career after he had announced his retirement. The event culminated in his trot around the ballpark as he shook hands with fans and waved goodbye. The fans responded with a five-minute standing ovation. He spoke with the same unpretentiousness that marked his career as he recalled his modest beginnings. "I'm just a potato farmer from Long Island who had some ability," he told the crowd. "I'm not any different than a mechanic or engineer or the president of a bank."[4]

By that time, a new future Hall of Famer had joined a Red Sox lineup that continued to replenish itself. And that was third baseman Wade Boggs, who emerged as one of the greatest pure hitters in baseball history. Boggs tormented opposing pitchers from the start with a .349 average as a rookie, then led the league in batting five of the next six years and in on-base percentage six of the next seven. He scored at least 100 runs in seven consecutive seasons. And though he managed double-figures in home runs just twice in his career, he was no singles hitter. Boggs was a doubles machine, slamming the ball into the gaps, down the lines, or off the Monster. He paced the American League in doubles in 1988 and 1989 and drilled at least 40 two-baggers every year between 1985 and 1991. The man who superstitiously ate chicken before every game and drew the Hebrew word for life in the ground during every at-bat (though he was not Jewish) used his bat like a magic wand, swatting line drives from foul line to foul line.

Boggs set a goal of two hits for every game. And though such a feat is impossible, he did average 211 hits in his first seven full seasons. "His work habits are unbelievable and he's got such high standards, too," said teammate Todd Benzinger. "I've seen him go two-for-four in a game and just be inconsolable in the clubhouse later because he didn't get a hit his last time up. His goals aren't to hit .300. He wants to hit .400. That's the reason he's so good—he's a perfectionist."[5]

But though Boggs was terrorizing pitchers, Jim Rice had reached his prime as an annual 100-RBI slugger, and Dwight Evans the hitter had caught up with Dwight Evans the brilliant outfielder, it was Clemens who provided the greatest hope for the future. The Red Sox had been desperately yearning for a premier starter since before Babe Ruth donned the pinstripes. Sure, pitchers such as Mel Parnell and Luis Tiant and Eckersley enjoyed fine seasons, but none had established himself as a consistent ace, let alone featured the same level of talent as that of Clemens. His brilliance raised confidence among fans, teammates, and Sox brass that the Curse of the Bambino was destined to be broken soon.

Perhaps the performance that best displayed that promise was his breakout effort of April 29, 1986. Clemens had shown flashes of his vast potential the previous two years but had now taken his rightful place as a healthy full-time starter. He had opened the season with three consecutive victories. But his control was a bit shaky and he had only struck out 19 in 24⅓ innings. The Sox welcomed Seattle to Fenway that night. The chilly temperatures and weak competition limited the crowd to a mere 13,414. It is quite likely that at least 50,000 now claim to have witnessed the event.

Few could have imagined that history would be made that evening when Clemens struck out the side in the first inning. But he continued to send frustrated Mariners back to the bench. He fanned three in the fourth and fifth to give him 12 for the game. He added two in each of the next three innings. Clemens had struck out 18 through eight. The major-league record was 19. Soon the mark was all his. He fanned Spike Owen,

Batting magician Wade Boggs considers where to place his next hit.
NATIONAL BASEBALL HALL OF FAME AND MUSEUM

his old college teammate whom he had twice brushed back to start the game, and Phil Bradley to start the ninth. Twenty strikeouts, zero walks. The fans roared their approval.

Clemens blurred the line between competitiveness and arrogance. Red Sox fans certainly viewed the personality of their new superstar more positively than players and followers of opposing teams. *Boston Globe* journalist Mark Starr wrote the following as he delved into the complexities of Clemens:

> *His competitiveness leads him to act like a jerk sometimes, and I don't admire that jerkiness or find it particularly appealing, but I love his intensity, love how visibly he cares. The old expression, "He wears it on his sleeve," applies. He does. . . . I like the emotions in Clemens. He's going to battle you. He'll come inside. He'll get himself tossed out of the game for the team.*[6]

Clemens quickly gained a reputation for boasting nasty pitches and a nasty demeanor. He became just the fifth pitcher in major-league history to win his first 14 decisions in 1986, earning the starting spot in the All-Star Game, during which he outpitched Mets phenom Dwight Gooden by retiring all nine batters he faced and snagging Most Valuable Player honors. But soon thereafter he became incensed over an unfavorable call in Chicago, charged the umpire, and bumped him. The automatic ejection angered him to the point that Rice and fellow teammate Don Baylor were forced to carry him off the field.

Both the greatness on the mound and orneriness off it continued to manifest themselves beyond the 24-4 season in 1986 that landed Clemens the American League Cy Young Award while also becoming the first starting pitcher to be named AL Most Valuable Player since Oakland's Vida Blue in 1971. Clemens also gained top pitcher honors in 1987 by leading the league with 20 victories, but not before he walked out of spring training over a contract dispute that Major League Baseball commissioner Peter Ueberroth was forced to settle.

Meanwhile, his professional relationships became more strained. After leading the Red Sox to a division crown in 1988 (they were swept by Oakland in the first round), he criticized management, teammates, and even Boston fans. He also complained about what most considered the wonderful trappings of athletic stardom, moaning over the need to travel and carry his own luggage, thereby alienating fans whose loathing of spoiled sports celebrities was growing with every multimillion-dollar contract.

Clemens emerged as the poster child for petulance while maintaining his brilliance. After a comparative down year in 1989, he won three straight ERA titles that included a career-best 1.93 in 1990 and a third Cy Young the next season. But he continued to make enemies. He was ejected in Game 4 of another four-game sweep against Oakland in the 1990 American League Championship Series when he began cursing out home plate umpire Terry Cooney over his interpretation of the strike zone. He charged Cooney and pushed fellow umpire Jim Evans to earn a fine and suspension. Three months later his anger got the best of him again when he was arrested at a Houston nightclub for preventing a security guard from stopping a fight involving older brother Randy.

His run of greatness in a Boston uniform ended in 1993. A barking pitching elbow hampered him early that year, as did a groin strain that landed him on the disabled list for a month. He lowered his ERA to 1.73 in mid-May, then allowed 30 earned runs in 41⅔ innings over his next six appearances before the shutdown. He performed well upon his return, but a dog bite on the right thumb sustained while trying to rescue a pooch he believed had been hit by a car continued his run of bad luck. He pitched miserably down the stretch, finishing the season with an 11-14 record and 4.46 ERA—nearly double that of his previous year. Despite flashes of brilliance, such as his second 20-strikeout game in the second of those years, general manager Dan Duquette weighed his 40-39 record and 3.76 ERA since 1993 and proclaimed Clemens to be in the "twilight" of his career. Though he made the right-hander an offer to keep him as free agency approached, Clemens believed it to be low enough to prove that he was no longer wanted.

Sox slugger and 1995 American League Most Valuable Player Mo Vaughn, who had signed a huge contract with the team in February 1996, complained the following year about a perceived hardball approach

Duquette had been taking in negotiations with Clemens. Also in disagreement was popular manager Kevin Kennedy, whom Duquette then fired in favor of Jimy Williams. The die was cast. Clemens signed a three-year contract with Toronto for more than $8 million per season. The deal easily trumped what was presented by Boston.

"I knew by their first, initial offer, by what Mr. Duquette put out there, that's in my heart, and I know my heart, that he really didn't want me back," said Clemens after hooking up with the Blue Jays. "Knowing that . . . didn't make this choice any easier. I'm extremely happy today. And deep down, he might tell you different, but I think he's happy."[7]

Duquette certainly proved premature with his assessment of Clemens. There was still a lot of sunshine left in his career, though it was marred by allegations of performance-enhancing drug use that prevented him through 2018 from gaining entrance into the Hall of Fame. Clemens twice led the American League in wins and ERA with Toronto before compiling a 77-36 record with the hated Yankees, pitching three years with Houston, then finishing his career in the Big Apple at age 45. He even won the ERA crown with the Astros well past his 40th birthday.

One wonders, given that the Sox placed second in the Eastern Division every year from 1998 to 2003, if keeping Clemens happy and at Fenway would have resulted in a first World Series title since 1918. But they remained strong throughout that period. And the long-coveted championship—as well as three others—was right around the corner.

CHAPTER SIXTEEN

Buckner's Boo-Boo

ONE CANNOT CLAIM THAT THE FLOOD OF FANS BESIEGING FENWAY Park in the late 1970s slowed to a trickle thereafter. But the Red Sox faithful certainly stopped showing up in force the next decade. Boston ranked fourth in American League attendance in 1980. After the strike-shortened 1981 season, the team tiered fifth, ninth, eighth, and seventh in the following years, respectively.

Carlton Fisk was gone. Fred Lynn was gone. Rick Burleson was gone. The good old days were gone. The manager was Ralph Houk, whose best seasons were so far behind him that they could barely be remembered. The former Yankees skipper hadn't won a pennant since 1964. In the 1960s and early 1970s he had guided that proud franchise to its first run of ineptitude in nearly a half-century, then managed the Tigers to four losing seasons in five before taking over the Sox. Among his failures in Boston was its first under-.500 record since 1966.

Not that Houk could be solely blamed. The offense aside from the outfield lacked punch during the Houk era and the pitching staff maintained its usual standing near the bottom of the American League. Personal issues contributed to the collapse of Dennis Eckersley, leaving the Sox without an ace until the healthy emergence of Clemens. Among the first moves made by aggressive new general manager Lou Gorman in 1984 was to trade Eckersley, who was set for free agency at the end of the season, to the Cubs for Bill Buckner. Little could Gorman have imagined that Eckersley would rebound to blossom into one of the greatest closers

First baseman Bill Buckner was a fine fielder and hitter but will forever be remembered for his error in 1986 World Series.
NATIONAL BASEBALL HALL OF FAME AND MUSEUM

in baseball history. The short-term results of the deal were sensational—at least until Buckner committed the most famous error of all time.

The addition of Buckner, as well as the emergences of power-hitting catcher Rich Gedman and third baseman Wade Boggs, who exploded onto the scene, had revitalized the Boston offense by 1984. The triumvirate of outfielders Jim Rice, Dwight Evans, and Tony Armas, along with slugging designated hitter Mike Easler, gave the Red Sox as dangerous a lineup as any in baseball. Only a lousy pitching staff that, oddly, featured three starters (Bruce Hurst, Oil Can Boyd, and Bob Ojeda) with identical 12-12 records prevented the team from contending.

It was the same sad story that plagued the team for generations. The powers-that-be in Boston often successfully compiled rosters that could bang the ball off the Monster and hit them over it while taking advantage of the short porch in right. But they could not find enough starters or relievers to stop opposing hitters from doing the same. And in an unlucky twist, when the Sox managed to assemble a decent staff in 1985, they lost Clemens to an injury while Easler and the outfielders all slumped. The result was a .500 record that had new manager John McNamara on the hot seat after just one season.

Red Sox fans gained few reasons for optimism heading into 1986. A gaping hole at shortstop remained—the likes of Rey Quiñones and Ed Romero had nobody turning cartwheels. And there was no reason to believe that pitching depth would be transformed from a weakness to a strength. Two players provided hope. A healthy Clemens boasted the talent not only to serve as a badly needed ace but to be a Cy Young candidate as well. And the addition of designated hitter Don Baylor might add offensive punch and leadership. Both of those factors proved vital in a possible charge to the top.

That charge began quickly. A 12-2 surge that included sweeps of Seattle and Oakland pushed the Sox into first place on May 11. Soon thereafter a 13-3 tear increased their lead to five games. They continued to win at a furious pace through June, after which they boasted a 50-25 record that inspired Gorman to add future Hall of Famer Tom Seaver for badly needed rotation depth beyond Clemens, Hurst, and Boyd. Seaver performed well in his first 10 starts before fading as he helped the Red Sox muddle through a slump that wiped out most of their lead. That slide coincided with the loss of the volatile Boyd, who threw a temper tantrum when his rejection of an All-Star selection cost him a $25,000 bonus. Boyd bolted the team and checked himself into a hospital for two weeks of observation, during which time the Boston advantage shrunk to 2½ games. Boyd revealed years later that he had used crack cocaine "every damn day" that season.[1]

The campaign began looking like the movie *Groundhog Day*—the Sox owned first place at the break in seven of the previous 14 years and had won just one pennant to show for it. The threat of blowing a lead that had once ballooned to eight games seemed quite real when they lost 14 of 19 as part of a 15-22 run that closed the gap to 3½ games on August 29. Then the Sox caught fire. While the Tigers and Yankees scuffled, they sizzled, winning 11 in a row to put away the American League East. McNamara rode the torrid bat of Rice and the arms of Clemens, Hurst, and Calvin Schiraldi to sweeps of Texas, Minnesota, and Milwaukee in a September surge that inspired fans to pack Fenway again.

The Red Sox cruised to the division crown, but Lady Luck did not seem to be smiling upon them as they prepared to meet the Angels for a World Series berth. They had lost five of their last six games in the regular season. Clemens was dealing with a sore elbow, the result of getting hit by a line drive in his last start against Baltimore, which knocked him out in the second inning. A strained right knee had sidelined Seaver, which meant that McNamara might be forced to start struggling Al Nipper in the playoffs, not a palatable option considering his 5.38 earned run average in the regular season. The blows of losing his mother after a long illness in late April and any chance to pitch in the playoffs devastated Seaver, who would never pitch another big-league inning, though he did not announce his retirement until the following June.

"It's the goal of any athlete to get to play in the postseason," he said. "I don't care how long you've played, it's why you work so hard all summer. This is definitely disappointing and frustrating. . . . One of the difficult things I'll have to deal with is that whatever success we have (in the playoffs), I will not have contributed to it physically. That's not easy to accept. . . . I came here at a time when Oil Can was having problems and Hurst was hurt, and I have to think that in my minor role I had significant impact on what the team was trying to achieve. But it's still been a very difficult year what with my mother dying, the sore arm I had in Chicago, then being traded into an environment that's been beneficial to me but now this, not being able to participate in the playoffs."[2]

The swelling in Clemens's elbow subsided enough to clear him for Game 1, but he pitched like he was still affected. After fanning the first two Angels in the second inning, he surrendered two walks, two singles, and a double. He settled down before getting knocked out in the eighth of an 8–1 defeat. The performance was worrisome. After all, if the Cy Young Award winner and Most Valuable Player failed, the Red Sox were doomed. Such a detestable destiny seemed inevitable after Game 4, in which Clemens and Schiraldi blew a 3–0 lead in the ninth, thanks partially to a misplay in left by Rice, then the latter yielded the game-winner in the 11th as Boston moved to within a game of elimination. Schiraldi was heartbroken. McNamara, who removed Clemens in the ninth in the belief that overexcitement caused poor pitches, had faith in his closer. This was no time for Schiraldi to end his successful save streak, which reached nine in the regular season. "It was the first time that I didn't do my job in that situation," he said. "I wanted the game, I wanted that situation, and I blew it."[3]

He did, but the Red Sox didn't. Their epic resilience turned the tables on Anaheim with an incredible ninth-inning rally in Game 5. Down 5–2 and with the Angels preparing to pop champagne, Baylor slugged a two-run homer that prompted manager Gene Mauch to give starter Mike Witt the hook and summon reliever Gary Lucas, who promptly hit Gedman. Reliable closer Donnie Moore then arrived on the mound to face late-season pickup Dave Henderson. The count reached 2-2. Red Sox pitcher Joe Sambito later described the scene as he witnessed it from the bullpen.

"The fans lined both sides of us, hooting at us, yelling at us, pointing," he recalled. "[Henderson] swung, and here came the ball toward us, and it went over the left-field fence and we all started cheering, but everyone else was stunned. The Angels fans were in utter silence. And then we started hooting at the fans. I mean, we got on them just as they were getting on us. I said to myself, 'How often do you see a game like that.'"[4]

The joy drained from Sambito soon after he arrived on the mound with a chance to clinch the victory. He allowed a game-tying single to light-hitting Rob Wilfong. The Angels loaded the bases with one out. They were again on the verge of winning the pennant but could not score the run from third. Henderson played hero again in the 11th with a sacrifice fly, then Schiraldi redeemed himself by retiring the side in order, striking out two to send the series to a sixth game.

Perhaps because of the frustration of blowing it one strike from the pennant for the Angels or the exhilaration of coming back from the dead for the Red Sox—or both—the ALCS had taken a dramatic turn that would not be reversed. Boston dominated Games 6 and 7 behind Boyd and Clemens, respectively, as well as the surprising productivity of Spike Owen, the ninth hitter who cranked out six hits of support as his team plated 18 runs. Boston could celebrate its first pennant since 1975. The New York Mets were the only obstacle to its first World Series championship in 68 years.

The Fall Classic featured two of the premier young fireballers in the sport—Clemens and Mets wunderkind Dwight Gooden, who remained lights-out as an ace in the pennant run. New York had dominated that season with a 108-54 record, leading the National League in runs scored and team earned run average along the way. And, unlike Boston, they had finished the regular season on a roll, winning nine of their last 10 games before burying Houston in six.

The Gooden-Clemens Clash of the Titans never materialized. The premier Sox moundsman was Hurst, who outpitched Mets starter Ron Darling in a taut opener with the help of Schiraldi for a 1–0 victory. Neither Clemens nor Gooden slogged through five innings the following night at Shea Stadium as Henderson continued to mash, slugging three of the team's 18 hits in a 9–3 victory that had some in Boston thinking sweep as the series hit Fenway. But former Boston starter Bob Ojeda, who had performed far better for the Mets after being swapped for Schiraldi after the 1985 season, stymied the Sox in Game 3. He spoke after the victory not about revenge or feeling bittersweet about beating his old teammates but rather about the competitive nature of baseball at its pinnacle. "It's competition out there," he said. "Everybody wants to knock everybody's socks off."

Ojeda had indeed knocked the Sox off to give the Mets momentum. McNamara hoped Nipper would nip that comeback in the bud, but the pitching matchup proved too unfavorable as he was clobbered by the Mets, who rode the talented arm of Darling to a victory that tied the series. One wondered if a home team would ever win a game, but they wondered no longer when Hurst outdueled Gooden the next day to place the Red Sox to within one victory of the ultimate championship.

October 25, 1986. It was a date known by Red Sox fans as vividly as July 4, 1776—just not celebrated. Those with the sharpest memories understand that the man who took the most blame for defeat in one of the greatest games in baseball history had plenty of company. Yes, Buckner went 0-for-5, flied out with the bases loaded in the eighth, and committed the error that cemented a Mets victory. But the Red Sox had already blown their lead and should have been celebrating a World Series crown by that time.

Inconsistent hurler Dennis "Oil Can" Boyd is all smiles here.
NATIONAL BASEBALL HALL OF FAME AND MUSEUM

Among the goats was Schiraldi, who relieved Clemens to start the eighth with a 3–2 lead. That he allowed a chop single to Lee Mazzilli through a gaping hole on the right side was no sin. But recklessly trying to force him at second and throwing wildly on a bunt certainly was. The eventual result was the tying run scored. And after the Sox scored two in the 10th on a home run by Henderson (who else?) and RBI single by Marty Barrett, who outperformed all the premier hitters on both teams in the series, Schiraldi blew it. With Boston one out away from victory and nobody on base, he surrendered three straight singles to cut the lead to 5–4 and motivate McNamara to summon Stanley, who then took the goat horns from his predecessor and shared them with Gedman. Stanley delivered a wild pitch to Mookie Wilson that could have been snagged by the catcher. It mattered not how the official scorer perceived it. The game was tied.

It seemed sadly appropriate that Stanley had yielded the tying run. It was a miserable ending to a miserable season for a closer who had once saved 33 games for the Red Sox. He had been booed all season by fans who resented his large contract and sudden struggles. So hated had he become by the bitterest of the faithful that one summer day he was berated by a driver that had pulled up next to him who became so irate at the sight of Stanley that he crashed his car at the next block. "That's OK," Stanley said when asked about his unpopularity. "When I'm on the mound in the World Series, they'll cheer me."[5]

They were not cheering in front of their TV sets. But the target of their anger and frustration shifted when Wilson chopped a dribbler down the first base line that flattened out as it reached Buckner, who failed to stay down. He lifted his glove as the ball scooted past and the winning run scooted home. Single, single, single, wild pitch, error, and it was over. Given the enormity of the moment, it was perhaps the most surreal ending in baseball history. And many Sox fans not superstitious enough to believe in the Curse of the Bambino became believers.

"It bounced and it bounced and then it didn't bounce," Bucker explained of his historic error. "It just skipped . . . I can't remember the last time I missed a ground ball. I'll remember this one."[6]

So would baseball fans forever—even those without rooting interests that fateful night. They would remember Game 6 with far more clarity than the one that decided the championship. And somehow it seemed the Sox were doomed even after homers by Evans and Gedman jump-started a three-run rally in the second inning and Hurst blanked the Mets on one hit through five. The southpaw collapsed in the sixth, motivating McNamara to pinch-hit for him and replace him with Schiraldi in the seventh. The disaster of a series continued for him as he allowed three runs in one-third of an inning. An Evans two-run double that closed the Boston deficit to 6–5 served only to heighten the frustration when the Mets staged a raucous victory celebration in front of the home fans.

In the end, Buckner would receive the historical blame. But it was the bullpen that deserved far more culpability for the painful defeat. The Red Sox relievers surrendered nine runs on 10 hits in the last 4⅔ innings they pitched over the final two games. They yielded 13 runs in 15⅓ innings for the series. They had snagged defeat from the jaws of victory. The result was that, like several generations before them and another after, this group of Red Sox would never experience the joy of winning a World Series for the baseball-crazed city of Boston. Among those who could hardly believe what he had experienced was Evans.

"I don't believe in luck," said the three-time All-Star. "I don't believe in history, either, but maybe I'm starting to."[7]

Evans, of course, was referring to the Curse of the Bambino. And after the 1986 World Series, that mysterious evil seemed stronger than ever.

CHAPTER SEVENTEEN

Ups and Downs with Nomar and Mo

THOSE WEREN'T IMPOSTERS SWINGING BATS FOR THE RED SOX IN THE early 1990s. They were really under contract. They just weren't the Red Sox to which fans had grown accustomed for generations. They weren't sending moonshots over the Monster. They weren't parading around the bases and wearing out home plate.

The power disappeared before the production. The home-run totals began fading in the pennant year of 1986 when the Sox placed a shocking 11th in the American League. They ranked no higher than ninth over the next eight seasons. It mattered not through the 1980s because they continued to batter opposing pitchers. Boston led one and all in runs scored in 1988 and 1989. But the offensive firepower for which the Red Sox had been identified since the Impossible Dream of 1967 disappeared in the early 1990s. They placed in the middle of the pack in runs in 1990 and 1991 before dropping to 13th, 12th, and 11th over the following three years, respectively.

The power guys and premier hitters were gone. Don Baylor had long since retired after a trade to Minnesota in 1987. Jim Rice called it quits in 1989. Dwight Evans, who got better with age, finally faded and was released in 1990. Wade Boggs was green-lighted for free agency after batting .259 in 1992—the anomaly amid 14 .300 averages in 15 seasons, which he continued with the archrival Yankees. Hard-hitting Ellis Burks was also granted his freedom and bolted for the White Sox.

Meanwhile, the pitching staff continued to lack depth beyond Clemens. General manager Lou Gorman supplemented his ace with capable veterans such as Mike Boddicker and Frank Viola while Jeff Reardon and Jeff Russell closed reliably. But young Aaron Sele was foolishly traded to Texas after two poor years and the Red Sox were left scrambling for rotation pieces by the end of the strike-shortened 1994 season. By that time they had posted three consecutive losing records for the first time since the 1960s, including a miserable 73-89 mark in 1992 that resulted in their first last-place finish in 60 years.

Few expected far better in 1995. Former Red Sox slugger Butch Hobson, who had taken over as manager in 1992 despite a distinct lack of credentials at that level, had been fired in favor of accomplished former Rangers skipper Kevin Kennedy. The death of owner Jean Yawkey (second wife of Tom Yawkey) had placed financial control of the franchise in a trust with her associate John Harrington running the team. Former Expos general manager Dan Duquette landed the same position under Harrington. But despite rib and groin injuries that sidelined prized free agent signing Jose Canseco, who was sent to the disabled list batting just .231 with one home run, the Sox finally provided optimism. The American League East was terrible—even the Yankees stumbled to a 16-25 start. Boston won nine of 10 in late May and early June to open a nine-game lead and still paced the division by four games in mid-July after a 16-22 run.

The Red Sox put the division away in early August with a 12-game winning streak that increased their lead to 10 games. They averaged more than seven runs during the blitz and never allowed over five. Fans flocked to Fenway. Every home game but one from late July to early September attracted at least 30,000 fans. A nine-game homestand against Cleveland, Baltimore, and New York all featured sellouts.

The drought was over. The Sox cruised to the American League East title. They had been upgraded from also-ran to division champion in one year. Kennedy received kudos for the transformation—some believed he deserved Manager of the Year honors over Seattle skipper Lou Piniella. Vaughn won Most Valuable Player, though he was statistically undeserving in comparison to Cleveland outfielder Albert Belle, whose surliness dearly cost him with voters in the media.

The far more understated acquisitions by Duquette and blossoming young players made the difference, though Canseco came on strong to hit .300 with 24 home runs in just 396 at-bats. Shortstop John Valentin boasted a career year with a .533 slugging percentage and 20 stolen bases. Duquette had plucked right-hander Tim Wakefield from oblivion after his release from Pittsburgh, and the knuckleballer paced the staff with 16 wins and a 2.95 ERA. Once-promising righty Erik Hanson proved a successful reclamation project with a 15-5 record. And closer Rick Aguilera, acquired on the verge of free agency from Minnesota for a career minor leaguer, saved 20 games in three months.

Awaiting in the American League Division Series was powerful Cleveland, for decades the laughingstock of the league and now a juggernaut. The Sox appeared on the verge of a road upset in Game 1 when third baseman Tim Naehring homered to break a tie in the 11th. But Aguilera blew it when Belle responded in kind leading off the bottom of the inning. Soon former Boston catcher Tony Peña was winning it for the Indians with a walkoff blast in the 13th.

The Red Sox never recovered. They were outscored 12–2 in the last two games to complete the sweep. Most disappointing is that Vaughn and Canseco combined to go 0-for-27 in the series with nine strikeouts—Vaughn alone fanned seven times in 14 at-bats. The pair stranded 17 baserunners. So desperate had Kennedy become for offense that he placed Canseco in the outfield for Game 3 and inserted Reggie Jefferson into the designated hitter spot. The stone-handed Canseco had played outfield just once since a ball bounced off his head and over the fence in a game, ironically, against Cleveland in 1993. The move didn't help, though Jefferson's one hit was one more than Vaughn and Canseco totaled in the series. And when it was over, Vaughn spoke like a man on a mission. "It will stick with me all winter the way this series went," he said. "I'll have to live with it. We'll learn something. I'll learn something."[1]

What the Sox learned in 1996 was that they needed far more help for Vaughn. They learned that Canseco couldn't stay healthy—he missed a month-and-a-half with a back injury. They learned that Valentin, though he remained a strong player, could not maintain the power production he displayed in 1995. And, most importantly, they learned that their pitching success the year before was merely a mirage. Not only did Clemens struggle through his fourth consecutive mediocre season, leading

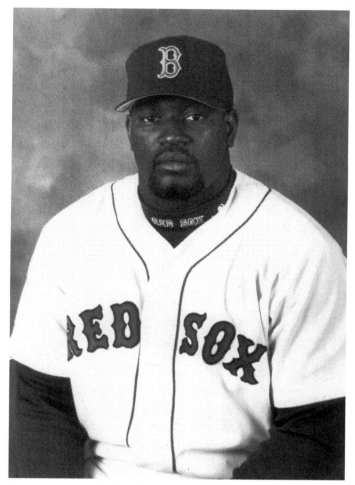

Home run basher Mo Vaughn won the 1995 American League MVP for Boston.
NATIONAL BASEBALL HALL OF FAME AND MUSEUM

Duquette to make his infamous claim that he was at the tail end of his career, but no other starter compiled an earned run average lower than 5.14. Wakefield and Tom "Flash" Gordon won more games than they lost due primarily to tremendous run support. Sele finished the season with a woeful WHIP of 1.646. Kennedy even handed 10 starts to the immortal

Vaughn Eshelman, who responded with a 7.08 ERA and horrific WHIP of 1.939.

Boston was not alone in its woes on the mound. With steroid use starting to run rampant, supposedly unknown to the powers-that-be, team ERAs of 5.00 or higher had grown commonplace. Combatants were clubbing each other to death with longballs. The Red Sox hit 209 home runs in 1996 yet finished sixth in the American League. Vaughn batted .326 with 44 home runs and 143 RBIs, but none of those numbers led the league and he placed only fifth in the Most Valuable Player balloting. He received some offensive help from Canseco when he was healthy, as well as catcher Mike Stanley and emerging outfielder Troy O'Leary. But a 6-19 start in which they allowed 6.5 runs per game pushed them 7½ games out in the East. A 27-10 run in August and early September catapulted them into wild card contention. That spot went to Baltimore as Boston finished third with an 85-77 record, prompting Duquette to fire Kennedy.

Kennedy was stunned by his dismissal a year after turning the team around and leading it to the playoffs. But the Sox had been dirtied by dissension. Kennedy had criticized their minor-league organization by claiming that young players were ill-prepared upon their arrival in The Show. He clashed over personnel decisions and pitching concerns with Duquette, who wanted him to give young players preference over the veterans that Kennedy preferred. "Our relationship was not one that was going to be productive for the team," Duquette said. "We have to have a cohesive management team up and down the organization. We didn't feel we were able to get everybody on the same page without a change."[2]

Meanwhile, the veterans detested Duquette's handling of contract negotiations, particularly those of outfielder Mike Greenwell and the disgruntled Clemens. So disenchanted was Greenwell that he cleared out his locker during the last week of the season with the Sox still alive in the playoff race and finished his career the following year in Japan.

It was all too much for Duquette. "It didn't help that the season ended the way it began," he said. "It was just abominable for me to see players clearing out their locker before the most important game of the season. That is just not acceptable in any operation."[3]

The results were an overhaul and new blood. The Sox hired as their manager Jimy Williams, who had failed to guide talented Toronto to the playoffs over the previous four seasons. Gone were Canseco, Clemens, and Greenwell. They let youth be served and it worked offensively with the contributions of emerging superstar Nomar Garciaparra, outfielder Wil Cordero, and flash-in-the-pan designated hitter Reggie Jefferson. The 1997 Sox ranked first in the American League in batting average and doubles and fourth in runs scored.

What Duquette failed to do was bolster a woeful pitching staff sans Clemens. So terrible was the bullpen that Williams was forced to move Tom Gordon, the only effective starter aside from Wakefield, into the closer role. Williams sent hopeful starter after hopeful starter to the mound in a vain attempt to catch lightning in a bottle as one and all ended up taking early showers. The Sox finished the season ranked 12th of 14 American League teams in ERA at 4.86. Their pathetic pitching more than outweighed the strong batting attack, resulting in an under-.500 record two years after the Sox reached the playoffs. Meanwhile, Clemens was winning 21 games and the first of two consecutive Cy Young Awards with the Blue Jays in a career rejuvenation (albeit rumored to have been aided by steroids) that lasted nearly a decade.

Among the few shining lights in a dark season was the unveiling of Garciaparra, whose brilliance at short and at the plate forced Williams to move Valentin and Jeff Frye into utility roles. Garciaparra sizzled early in the season, hitting safely in 17 of 18 games in late April and early May, cooled off, then embarked on a torrid blitz in the heat of the summer. He batted .383 during a 30-game hitting streak that established a major-league rookie record. He slugged nine home runs and scored 35 times during that tear. His 209 hits led the American League. That he received all 28 first place votes for American League Rookie of the Year proved to be as big a surprise as the sun rising in the east.

The Californian who often phoned his batting instructor father Ramon ("Nomar" backward) for advice was embraced by Red Sox fans seeking a new hero upon the departure of Clemens, though some have claimed Vaughn would have filled that void had he not been African American. Legendary Red Sox shortstop Johnny Pesky praised

Garciaparra, claiming that he himself would have been sitting on the bench had the talent of the latter worn a Boston uniform in the 1940s and 1950s. "He's the best shortstop I've ever seen and the best we've ever had," offered Pesky, who slammed 200-plus hits in each of his first three seasons.[4]

Garciaparra continued to perform at a Hall of Fame level with incredible consistency. He led the AL in batting in 1999 and 2000, peaking at an absurd .372 in the second of those seasons. He finished among the top five in Most Valuable Player balloting five times from 1998 to 2003. He exceeded 100 runs scored in all six full seasons with Boston and four times drove in more than 100. Five years after he was shockingly swapped for nondescript first baseman Doug Mientkiewicz and shortstop Orlando Cabrera in 2004, he finished his career with a .313 average.

That trade might not have been consummated had Garciaparra remained healthy. He was ravaged by injuries, including a split tendon in his wrist and a groin injury. He never played a full season after 2003, though he did stay on the field long enough for the Dodgers in 2006 to earn Comeback Player of the Year honors. Three years later he retired with not enough in the statistical arsenal to be considered for the Hall of Fame. Those that watched him play in his prime believed he was destined for Cooperstown.

The greatness of Garciaparra inspired natural comparisons with Yankees superstar shortstop Derek Jeter. But his muscular appearance on the cover of *Sports Illustrated* had some speculating whether the physical breakdown that followed was related to steroids. Among those who wondered was *Boston Globe* columnist Bob Ryan, who wrote the following after Garciaparra had been traded:

Look, I'm hardly the first person to raise the question. When he was with the Red Sox, who was bold enough to link our fair shortstop, a noted workout guy, with the dreaded S-word? But he did go from, like, standard athlete issue normal to ultra-buffed in one winter, and he has been—there is no other way to say it—systematically breaking down for the past six years, so you can't help wondering just what he's been putting into his body other than Wheaties and sirloin steaks. If

Superstar shortstop Nomar Garciaparra really raked for the Red Sox in the 1980s.
NATIONAL BASEBALL HALL OF FAME AND MUSEUM

we're going to assume that Mark McGwire's physical breakdown was because of a reliance on steroids, then it would be quite logical to adopt the same line of thinking about Nomar.[5]

Garciaparra scoffed at the accusation, but the steroid era left many questions unanswered. Red Sox fans had few regrets when the 2004 team cast aside the Curse of the Bambino and won it all. But one of them was that Garciaparra was sent packing before he could experience the triumph he had dreamed about ever since donning a Boston uniform.

CHAPTER EIGHTEEN

A Little Big Mistake

THE RED SOX WERE SANS ACE FOR ONE YEAR UPON THE DEPARTURE OF
Roger Clemens in 1997. Presumably wearing a mask and holding a gun,
general manager Dan Duquette pulled highway robbery on the Montreal
Expos after that season when he stole emerging superstar right-hander
Pedro Martínez in exchange for not-ready-for-prime-time pitcher Carl
Pavano and nondescript hurler Tony Armas, whose namesake father once
starred in a Boston uniform.

Martínez was simply the premier pitcher of his generation. During a
steroid era in which even the best struggled to maintain under-4 earned
run averages, he kept the ball in the park and led the league with micro-
scopic ERAs such as 1.90 (1997), 2.07 (1999), 1.74 (2000), 2.26 (2002),
and 2.22 (2003). Others could throw fastballs with equal velocity, but
the late movement on his wicked breaking balls had batters flailing away
in vain. Martínez five times averaged 9.9 strikeouts or more per nine
innings, peaking when he fanned 313 in just 213 innings in 1998. It was
no wonder that he landed in the Hall of Fame on the first ballot in 2015.

The acquisition of Martínez and the six-year, $75 million contract
that followed certainly proved wise, but it ruffled some Red Sox feathers,
especially those of Mo Vaughn, who had been seeking in vain a similar
deal from Duquette. Among the rumored reasons that such an offer was
never made to the slugger was that CEO John Harrington did not appre-
ciate his off-field habits, such as his propensity to visit strip clubs. Though
acquitted of the charges, Vaughn had been accused of punching a man
in the face at a Cleveland strip joint a year earlier. He accused Duquette

Almost unhittable Pedro Martínez won four ERA titles in a Boston uniform.
NATIONAL BASEBALL HALL OF FAME AND MUSEUM

of hiring a private detective to follow him around. Contract negotiations played out in the media resulted in an insulting four-year offer for just $37 million.

The Red Sox could claim whatever they wished about Vaughn's nightlife and eating habits that caused him to remain out of shape, but they could not complain about his production. While they low-balled him in contract haggling in 1998, he continued to mash. He enjoyed perhaps his finest season, batting a career-high .337 with 40 home runs. He finished in the top five in American League Most Valuable Player voting for the third time in four seasons.

Meanwhile, Martínez proved himself the second coming of Clemens as a badly needed ace. His stuff drew raves. Comparing his statistics to other starters given the offensive explosions and bloated earned run averages of the steroid era, some believe he was the greatest pitcher in baseball history at his peak. His competitive fire combined with maddening movement on his breaking balls had American League hitters as frustrated as their National League counterparts. He finished the 1998 season at 19-7 with a 2.89 ERA. And that was an off-year—the only one between 1997 and 2000 that he didn't lead the league in ERA and WHIP and win the Cy Young Award.

"He's the most dominant pitcher I've seen in my 26 years," praised Red Sox pitching coach Joe Kerrigan. "He's so devastating. He can play a power game with you and can also play a finesse game when he doesn't have his number one fastball. He's the most complete package you'll see."[1]

The Red Sox fell helplessly behind the juggernaut Yankees by late May but earned a wild card berth. Vaughn caused a bit of a distraction with a week remaining in the regular season by announcing his plan to test the free agent waters, but such a decision had been expected. The trade for Martínez (as well as the solid pitching of Tim Wakefield and rejuvenation of veteran right-hander Bret Saberhagen) began paying off in earnest when he pitched the team to a Game 1 victory over Cleveland to end its 13-game playoff losing streak. He was expected to pitch Game 4 after Boston lost the next two to place itself on the brink of elimination, but manager Jimy Williams opted for nondescript southpaw Pete

Schourek over Martínez on short rest. Schourek performed brilliantly, but Williams was not off the hook for criticism. He summoned Tom Gordon to hold a 1–0 lead in the eighth inning, during which the closer had never pitched all season. Gordon boasted 43 consecutive saves, but he could not lock down that one. He allowed two singles and a double that scored two runs. The lead was lost, the game was lost, the season was lost, and Vaughn was lost.

The Sox could not replace him. Mike Stanley took over at first in 1999 and compiled a fine .393 on-base percentage. The reduction of power in a longball era proved to be pronounced. Boston ranked ninth in the American League in runs scored and home runs that year. That the Red Sox reached the playoffs was a testament to Martínez, who embarked on one of the greatest seasons ever. The incredible achievement of a 23-4 record paled in comparison to that of his 2.07 ERA considering that the Yankees' David Cone placed second in the AL that year with a 3.44 mark.

Martínez peaked in late August and September with the Sox trying in vain to chase down the first-place Yankees or at least secure the wild-card spot. He won all six decisions, allowing five runs in 56 innings covering seven starts. His most impressive performance of the season was a one-hitter at Yankee Stadium on September 10 in which he struck out 17. Cone called it "the best-pitched game I've ever seen . . . I've never seen anything better." He added that Martínez boasted "three completely dominant pitches, a great fastball, a knee-buckling curve and a parachute changeup. Other than that, what else do you need? . . . He did it here, in Yankee Stadium, in a pennant race, when the team really needed a win."[2]

The team certainly needed a win in a revenge battle against the Indians. The Sox were on the precipice of a three-game sweep when a back injury knocked Martínez out after he'd pitched four shutout innings in a Game 1 loss, then Saberhagen was mashed in an 11–1 defeat the next night. But the offense came to life at Fenway. The Sox exploded for 32 runs in Games 3 and 4, including 23 in the latter, as John Valentin slammed three home runs and drove in 10. Saberhagen was again clobbered in the deciding battle in Cleveland, but the Red Sox bats continued to sizzle. The game was tied at 8–8 heading into the bottom of the fourth. That is when Martínez shocked the baseball world by returning to the mound—bad back and all. He pitched no-hit ball for six innings and Troy O'Leary slugged two home runs and drove in seven as Boston clinched a pennant showdown against (who else?) the Yankees. Martínez admitted after the brilliant performance that he had placed his career in jeopardy by pitching with a strained back. He had placed team over self.

But the Curse of the Bambino had yet to be lifted. The Red Sox received some satisfaction in Game 3 when they creamed Clemens in another shutout effort by Martínez, but that proved to be their lone victory. Boston was outscored 15–3 over the last two games at Fenway to exit with a whimper.

The uncharacteristic lack of offensive firepower and zero pitching depth beyond Martínez and closer Derek Lowe doomed the Red Sox to early vacations the next three years. They did show signs of life on both fronts under new manager Grady Little in 2002, however, as Garciaparra, previous-year acquisition Manny Ramírez, and outfielder Trot Nixon combined for 81 home runs and 321 RBIs to raise the Red Sox to second in the American League in runs scored, while the return of Lowe to the starting rotation gave the team two 20-game winners for the first time since Mel Parnell and Ellis Kinder in 1949. Lowe's closer role was placed in the capable hands of veteran Ugueth Urbina, who saved 40 games.

A 26-30 late-season slide prevented the Sox from reaching the post-season, but they would not be denied in 2003. The batting attack flourished as several Sox enjoyed career years, thanks greatly to shrewd moves by new general manager Theo Epstein. Among them was the acquisition of second baseman Todd Walker, who was stolen in a lopsided swap with Cincinnati and drove in a career-high 85 runs. Garciaparra and outfielder Trot Nixon managed their last productive seasons in Boston. Designated hitter David Ortiz, who was released by a shortsighted Twins front office that considered him a platoon player, launched a love affair with Red Sox Nation by totaling 31 home runs and 101 RBIs. Epstein found lightning in a bottle with his purchase from the Marlins of first baseman Kevin Millar, who managed career-highs with 25 home runs and 96 RBIs. The Sox bashed foes into oblivion with 238 home runs and a league-best six runs per game. Incredibly, eight of their nine regular position players drove in at least 85 runs, including previously unproductive nondescript infielder Bill Mueller, who paced the circuit with a .326 batting average.

The offensive explosion allowed the Red Sox pitching staff to retreat to their more traditional standing of mediocrity. Martínez again dominated with a 2.22 ERA and might have won a fourth Cy Young Award had he not missed a month with a shoulder injury. But fellow starters such as Wakefield, Lowe, and John Burkett could all thank run support for their winning records despite average-to-poor earned run averages.

That weak pitching prevented Boston from wresting the division crown away from New York. The Sox pulled to within 1½ games of the lead in early September with successive wins at Yankee Stadium before falling back for their sixth of eight consecutive second-place finishes and set up one of the most memorable and controversial playoff runs in team history. A revenge match against the Yankees could only be achieved by an American League Division Series defeat of the Oakland Athletics, who gained greater fame years later as the subject of the film *Moneyball*, which all but ignored the fact that the team finished a mere ninth in the junior circuit in runs scored and led one and all in team earned run average. The Sox would be challenged by an excellent starting trio of Tim Hudson, Barry Zito, and Mark Mulder, as well as lights-out closer Keith Foulke, who paced the AL with 43 saves.

That staff appeared destined to sweep aside the Sox with two victories in Oakland to start the series. But Lowe and relievers Mike Timlin and late procurement Scott Williamson shut down the A's in Game 3, allowing Nixon to win it in the 11th with a walkoff home run. The slumping Ortiz played hero the next day, slamming a two-run double in the eighth to complete a comeback and tie the best-of-five with a deciding showdown set for the following night. With Martínez struggling a bit more than usual on the mound, the bats came to life in a four-run sixth inning, courtesy of Manny Ramírez and steady catcher Jason Varitek, who had enjoyed his most productive season. Both bashed homers to give Boston a lead it would not relinquish and a trip to the ALCS against the Bronx Bombers. Another opportunity awaited to vanquish the Curse.

The 2003 Sox embraced the rodeo term "Cowboy Up" to define their toughness. The maxim was first adopted by Timlin, Millar, and Nixon, then by the entire team. "'Cowboy Up' is just an expression," Timlin explained. "You've been knocked down, get up. Yeah, you're bleeding, you're hurt, but get up and keep going." Added Millar: "It's the old wives' tale of the cowboy being a tough guy and getting stomped on. Hey man, you're not feeling good? Get out there and cowboy up. It's been a fun little motto for the team."[3]

The victory over Oakland inspired a reaction usually reserved for greater triumphs. Beantowners went wild. Two sisters were hauled away by cops for exposing their breasts. Fans overturned cars and set them on fire. Two thousand revelers at the University of Massachusetts rioted. Sox loyalists broke into Fenway Park and raced about the field until shooed away by the city's finest. The celebrations seemed over the top given that their team had yet to win the pennant. But the mere thought of upending the hated Yankees motivated merriment.

The need for Martínez to pitch the clincher forced Little to schedule him for Game 3. A showdown with Clemens awaited as the teams split the first two in New York with Ramírez and Ortiz both homering in the opener. The fan hatred of the Yankees reached a fever pitch as the series returned to Fenway and the nastiness permeated the playing field. An inning after Martínez fired a fastball that plunked Karim Garcia in the shoulder, Clemens retaliated by nearly hitting Ramírez. Both benches cleared. Yankees coach and former Red Sox manager Don Zimmer made a beeline toward Martínez, who grabbed the 72-year-old by the neck and shoulders and pulled him to the ground. Incensed New York catcher Jorge Posada screamed at Martínez, who responded by warning, "The next time, I'm going to hit you in the head."[4]

Even a Fenway groundskeeper was not immune to the tumult. Sent out to smooth the mound in the ninth inning, he felt compelled to exhort the Sox to victory by waving his towel. Yankees reliever Jeff Nelson and Garcia attacked the worker, who ended up in the hospital. All three were charged with assault two months later. Making matters worse for Martínez, he suffered his first postseason defeat and was fined $50,000.

Soon Wakefield emerged as a Sox savior. His knuckleball baffled the hard-swinging hitters in a Game 4 victory in which he allowed just one run in seven innings. The Sox were placed on the brink of elimination the next day when a three-run second inning doomed Lowe to defeat. And when starter John Burkett got clobbered in Game 6 and the Red Sox fell behind 6–3 heading into the seventh inning, all seemed lost. But Boston battled back, piecing together a four-run rally launched by a Garciaparra triple and Ramírez double to take the lead and hanging on for dear life to send the series into a dramatic, deciding Game 7 at Yankee Stadium.

The sigh of relief over the four-hit performance by Garciaparra could be heard in Maine. The slumping slugger had batted just .170 in September and lowered that mark to .105 in the championship series. He had blown several opportunities with runners in scoring position, leading the *Boston Globe* to speculate that he was "hurt, tired, or preoccupied with his wedding to [soccer superstar] Mia Hamm next month" and radio station WEEI to make the seemingly ridiculous proposition that he should be benched in favor of career reserve Lou Merloni. One major-league scout claimed the following to *Globe* sportswriter Gordon Edes:

"His bat's slow, he looks like he's guessing wrong, he looks sluggish. That's how it looks when you're struggling, but that's what I see, a slower bat. I don't know if it's just because he's in a funk, or something else is going on. Obviously, he's not the same. He doesn't have the quick trigger. Usually he's a dead-red, first-ball fastball hitter. If you throw something in the zone hard, he's going to hit it hard somewhere. That pitch he struck out on against Wells [with two on and two out in the third inning of Game 5], that's normally a pitch he would smoke. I don't know why his bat is slow, but it's not getting in the [hitting] zone like it normally does."[5]

The finale would give Garciaparra and his fellow Sox a chance to not only quiet the naysayers but upend a Yankees team that had been a thorn in their side for generations. The epic matchup was set: Martínez vs. Clemens. But only the former was on top of his game. Home runs by Nixon and Millar knocked Rocket Roger out in the fourth. Meanwhile, Martínez was mowing down the Yankees, allowing only one run until Jason Giambi homered in the seventh. Two singles followed, indicating that the Boston ace was tiring, but he escaped the jam and entered the eighth with a 5–2 lead.

He had thrown 115 pitches. It had been well established that the lithe, but live-armed Martínez lost effectiveness after throwing 100 to the plate. The bullpen featuring Timlin, Williamson, Alan Embree, and Bronson Arroyo had performed well in the series. Millions wondered why Little had not summoned one of them to the mound. Their cries grew louder as the inning progressed. Martínez retired the first batter, but then allowed a double to Derek Jeter and run-scoring single to Bernie Williams. Surely Little would remove Martinez now—but no. All he did was pay a visit to his pitcher—who assured him as usual he wanted to remain in the game—and returned to the dugout. Hideki Matsui followed with a double that placed the tying run in scoring position. Surely Little would remove Martinez now—but no. Not until Martinez surrendered a two-run single to Jorge Posada did he mercifully call for Timlin.

The manager believed Martínez was fine, later asserting that he had gotten two strikes on all five batters that reached base and was still firing his fastball close to the mid-90s. But what did not seem obvious to Little certainly seemed obvious to the rest of the baseball world and every Red Sox fan wanting to throw their TV sets out the window. Boston fan and poet James Bair captured the frustrations of one and all with a poem of wonderment over the inaction of Little. The following two stanzas expressed the maddening thoughts about the manager, even dredging up the name of long-since deceased Sox owner Harry Frazee and his sale of Babe Ruth to the Yankees:

> We couldn't have got there without you.
> We were five outs away from a win.
> You were the smartest guy in the stadium.
> But why did you keep Pedro in?
> We don't believe in curses.
> We could care less about old Harry's sin.
> But with such a powerful bullpen.
> Why did you keep Pedro in?[6]

It seemed that the Curse of the Bambino had reared its ugly head at Yankee Stadium and would refuse to leave until it had doomed the Sox again. The game came down to a battle between Timlin and New York super closer Mariano Rivera. Little summoned Wakefield, who hurled a perfect 10th inning before facing Aaron Boone to start the 11th. Boone had faded after two strong seasons in Cincinnati. Memories of Bucky Dent raced through the minds of fatalistic fans. And, sure enough, Boone slammed a Wakefield knuckleball into the left field stands. Game over. Season over.

The championship drought was 85 years and counting. And soon Little, who had made one terrible decision in a season in which he made so many right ones, was sent packing in favor of former Phillies manager Terry Francona.

Twenty-three years earlier, legendary sportscaster Al Michaels had famously asked American sports fans the question, "Do you believe in miracles?" Red Sox fans did not in November 2003. But that miracle millions had died waiting for was about to come.

CHAPTER NINETEEN

Big Papi and the Big Comeback

TWINS GENERAL MANAGER TERRY RYAN FIGURED POWER-HITTING, poor-fielding platoon first basemen were a dime a dozen. And he had one in David Ortiz. The large Dominican had spent six seasons in the Minnesota organization and played almost exclusively against right-handed pitching. He could send balls into orbit, but impending arbitration eligibility and the promise of young slugger Justin Morneau motivated Ryan to attempt in vain to trade Ortiz, then release him after the 2002 season, a move he would lament forever. Ryan's crystal ball proved faulty. "It was just a bad error in judgment of a guy's talent," Ryan later admitted.[1]

New Boston general manager Theo Epstein was intrigued. So were Sox scouts Louie Eljaua and Jesus Alou. They all believed Ortiz would be an upgrade over the duo of Tony Clark and Brian Daubach, who had served as the first base platoon that year. Also chiming in was statistical guru Bill James, who had joined the front office and encouraged Epstein to sign Ortiz. The brain trust did not promote Ortiz simply for his ability to hit a baseball deep into the night.

"Everybody was in favor of signing David Ortiz," James said. "I liked him because of his numbers, the scouts liked him because of his swing, [and] some people liked him because they knew he was a positive guy in the clubhouse."[2]

Each of those assessments proved accurate, but little could anyone have imagined to what extent. Ortiz blossomed into a surefire Hall of Famer as mostly a designated hitter not only for smashing 541 home runs, including 483 in a Red Sox uniform, and producing 10 100-plus-RBI seasons

Beloved Sox slugger David Ortiz hits one sky-high but foul against Baltimore.
WIKIMEDIA COMMONS

but also for his leadership and personality that made him one of the most beloved players in franchise history. After spending 2003 as a platoon player under Little, new manager Terry Francona showed the foresight to start him against both right-handers and southpaws. Ortiz soon emerged as the most significant figure in the greatest era of Red Sox baseball.

The hiring of Francona, who had been serving as an Athletics bench coach, proved eventful as well. But it was another acquisition made soon thereafter that provided a second superstar in the rotation. And that was pitcher Curt Schilling, who signed a two-year contract with an option for a third that would exceed $38 million. The two moves were intertwined. So impressed was Schilling with Francona, who had managed the right-hander with the Phillies, that he was inspired to join the Red Sox. Like a fine wine, Schilling got better with age. Plagued by injury and inconsistency most of his career, he had blossomed in his mid-30s with Arizona, winning 45 games in 2001 and 2002 combined and compiling his lowest earned run average since 1992 a year later. A fierce competitor, Schilling was also motivated by the Red Sox–Yankees rivalry. So excited were Red Sox fans over his signing and the prospects for a special year that they sold out Fenway for the season before it began.

Schilling proved to be the missing piece in a championship puzzle in 2004, especially since Martínez struggled for the first time since the trade to Boston, nearly doubling his ERA to 3.90. A big year from closer Kevin Foulke, who had departed Oakland in free agency, and a powerful lineup that led the American League in doubles, batting average, on-base percentage, slugging percentage, and runs scored allowed fellow starters Tim Wakefield, Bronson Arroyo, and Derek Lowe to thrive as well. Ortiz and Manny Ramírez, who combined to smash 84 home runs and drive in 269, received plenty of support from talented veteran outfielder Johnny Damon, flash-in-the-pan second baseman Mark Bellhorn, first baseman Kevin Millar, and catcher Jason Varitek.

Yet many among the fans that besieged the oldest ballpark in Major League Baseball wanted their money back well into the season. The 2004 Red Sox edition seemed no better than those that graced Fenway before them. They proved maddeningly inconsistent into mid-August, unable to maintain long winning streaks or embarking on long win-one, lose-one stretches. The result was a disappointing 64-52 record that placed them 10½ games out of first place and seemingly hopelessly behind the Yankees in the race for the American League East crown.

By that time Garciaparra was gone. He had been hurt emotionally by an offseason trade proposal that would have sent Ramírez to Texas for Alex Rodriguez, who would have replaced him at short. And he had been hurt physically by a groin injury that had prevented him from joining the lineup until June 9. Garciaparra had descended the previous two seasons from otherworldly to mere All-Star, and his production continued to fall in 2004. Trade rumors began to surface. Most believed the Sox could negotiate a fine haul for Garciaparra, who despite his slide still scored and drove in more than 100 runs in 2002 and 2003. But when the dust had

Terry Francona broke the Curse and led the Sox to two World Series crowns.
WIKIMEDIA COMMONS

settled, he had been dealt to the Cubs in a three-team deal that only netted first baseman Doug Mientkiewicz and shortstop Orlando Cabrera. The former had earned a sterling reputation for his glove and a weak one for his bat. The latter provided a decent half-year for the Sox and walked in free agency after the season.

The Red Sox banished Garciaparra, who had been criticized by some in the media as a me-first athlete who had become unhappy in Boston, with an eye to the future. Young phenom Hanley Ramírez was soon promoted to Triple-A as his heir apparent at shortstop. Ramírez did not spend a day with the Sox until a late-career stint that began in 2015, but his vast talents were parlayed in a trade to the Marlins into brilliant right-hander Josh Beckett and third baseman Mike Lowell, whose sensational 2007 season played a huge role in the securing of another World Series crown.

The Sox stumbled along after Garciaparra was sent packing. But then they caught fire. They swept the Blue Jays, White Sox, Tigers, Angels, and

Athletics during a 20-2 tear that took baseball by storm and catapulted them to within two games of the division lead. A three-game losing streak that included two defeats at Yankee Stadium destroyed hopes of an East championship, but Boston won seven of nine to end the regular season on a roll. With Martínez, Schilling, and Arroyo all performing well in their respective starts and Damon, Ortiz, and Ramírez leading an attack that scored 25 runs, the Red Sox rolled past Anaheim in a three-and-out American League Division Series for yet another pennant showdown against New York.

The Sox were not the only team seeking a World Series berth that had vastly improved their roster in the offseason. The Yankees added veteran starting pitcher Kevin Brown. But far more significant was a swap that landed Rodriguez, perhaps the premier all-around hitter in the sport, though he slumped a bit in his first year in the Big Apple, batting just .286 with 36 home runs and 106 RBIs. It marked the worst season of his career until he hit his mid-30s.

Boston fans that had grown impatient (to put it mildly) for their team to smash the Curse wanted to smash a vase or lamp after watching Yankees ace Mike Mussina hurl a perfect game through six innings of the opener after Schilling got knocked out after three. Many a TV set in Beantown had been turned off before the Sox staged a spirited comeback launched after Bellhorn broke up the perfect game with a double in the seventh. Varitek capped the five-run rally with a two-run homer, then a two-run triple by Ortiz in the eighth closed the deficit to 8–7.

But it was as if the Curse was simply teasing the Sox and their tortured faithful. They lost that game, then collapsed at Yankee Stadium in Game 2, during which they managed just five hits. The Bronx Bombers simply bombed Boston into submission in Game 3. The Sox hung around for a while—the score was tied at 6–6 through three innings—but the New York bullpen stemmed the tide while the tide washed over their counterparts. When the massacre had been completed, the Fenway scoreboard displayed the grisly truth: Yankees 19, Red Sox 8. Sox pitchers had been pounded for 22 hits, only nine of which were singles. Boston had lost to New York in the playoffs before, lord knows, but had never been humiliated like that.

Defeat seemed a foregone conclusion. Francona contended his team was not done. But he had to say that. It was assumed the Sox were cooked. No team in baseball history had overcome a 3–0 series deficit. The evil Curse had them in a chokehold. The only folks that claimed not to believe it wore Red Sox uniforms. Among them was Kevin Millar. "Don't let us win tonight," he said. "This is a big game. They've got to win because if we win we've got Pedro coming back . . . and then Schilling will pitch Game 6 and then you can take that fraud stuff and put it to bed. Don't let the Sox win this game."[3]

What to everyone else was inevitable appeared to be on the doorstep in the ninth inning of Game 4. The Yankees led 4–3 with Closer of the Universe Mariano Rivera on the mound. But then something strange and unexpected happened. Rivera, who walked two batters per nine innings throughout his career, issued a leadoff freebie to Kevin Millar. Pinch-runner Dave Roberts, showing the balls of a burglar, stole second on the first pitch to Mueller, who smashed a single up the middle to forge a 4–4 tie. Foulke and bullpen mates Mike Timlin, Alan Embree, Mike Myers, and Curt Leskanic held New York scoreless through the 12th. Rivera was long gone when Ortiz lined a Paul Quantrill fastball he was expecting for a game-winning home run to right that kept the Sox breathing. Barely.

One could sense a seismic shift. That shift might have been dismissed as a mental mirage when Jeter hit a three-run double off Martínez in the sixth inning of Game 5 to give New York a 4–2 lead. But Ortiz was far from done hitting his way into the hearts of Red Sox fans. He homered leading off the eighth to start a rally that knotted the score. The bullpen again shut down a vaunted Yankees attack through the 14th inning, when Ortiz (who else?) blooped a single to center that sent the series back to the Big Apple. The legend of Big Papi was growing.

The Red Sox carried their momentum to New York and ran with it. Schilling, who was clobbered in the opener and was suffering from an ankle injury, courageously toed the rubber in Game 6 and allowed just one run through seven innings. Television cameras focused on blood soaking through his right sock. And though some—mostly bitter Yankee fans—have called it the "ketchup sock," claiming the right-hander had doctored it to bolster his image, the reality of what millions of viewers witnessed gained a greater sense of truth 10 years later when Schilling tweeted an old photo of how gnarly the ankle looked in the fall of 2004. The bloody sock emerged as a symbol of Sox resolve in returning from the dead in the ALCS. The Schilling performance allowed a four-run fourth inning highlighted by a three-run homer from Bellhorn to stand up and tie the series at 3–3.

The date was October 20. The venue was Yankee Stadium. The event was Game 7 of the American League Championship Series. The ritual was the breaking of the Curse of the Bambino. Never mind that the Red Sox still required a World Series victory over the Cardinals to end their 86-year drought. It felt like the 10–3 mashing of Kevin Brown and the Yankees that fateful night behind the pitching of Lowe and four home runs, including another from Ortiz, had finally, mercifully ended the jinx. *Boston Globe* sportswriter Dan Shaughnessy expressed the feelings of Sox fans with the following after the deed had been done.

> *On the very soil where the Sox were so cruelly foiled in this same game one year ago, the Sons of Tito Francona completed the greatest postseason comeback in baseball history. No major league team had ever recovered from a 3–0 series deficit.*
>
> *Red Sox fans now have a stock answer for those clever chants of "1918." They'll always be able to cite the fall of 2004 when the Big Apple was finally and firmly lodged in the throats of men wearing pinstripes. This time, it was the gluttonous Yankees who choked.[4]*

Boston would not lose another game until 2005. A three-run homer by Ortiz allowed Bellhorn to win Game 1 of the Fall Classic with a two-run blast in the ninth, and the Red Sox never looked back. Schilling, Martínez, Lowe, and the Boston bullpen held the potent Cardinals to just three runs over the last three games combined while Mueller, Bellhorn, Ortiz, Ramírez, and Damon provided enough offense to doom the Cardinals in four straight. The Curse had been lifted in New York, but the drought had ended at Busch Stadium.

"This is what we've all been waiting for," crowed general manager Theo Epstein. "We can die happy. I just hope everyone out there who has been rooting for the Red Sox the last eighty-six years is enjoying this as much as we are. We're coming home to see you soon."[5]

The victory parade that attracted an estimated 3.2 million people representing Red Sox Nation was among the largest crowd events in Boston history. The players waved at fans as they rode by in duck boats and the fans waved back as they uttered the two most-spoken words to their heroes that day: "Thank you."[6]

Sox fans would happily grow accustomed to voicing those same sentiments over the next 14 years.

CHAPTER TWENTY

Manny Being Manny

THE LEGACY OF MANNY RAMÍREZ SHOULD SPOTLIGHT A SWEET POWER stroke that made him arguably the greatest pure hitter of his generation. But instead, he will forever be remembered for his flaky personality, gaffes in the outfield, and steroid use that could forever prevent him from entering the hallowed halls in Cooperstown despite statistics that warrant first-ballot admission.

Ramírez had earned a reputation as a space cadet well before his ballyhooed free agent signing as an early Christmas present for Sox fans in 2000. After all, who else would leave his paycheck in a boot in the visitor's clubhouse or get thrown out stealing first, as Ramírez did in 1997 when he jogged back to that bag after swiping second in the mistaken belief that the pitch had been fouled off?

But those that believed Ramírez lacked focus ignore what has been described as genius and studious foresight at the plate. Pitchers have claimed that he would pretend to be fooled by an offering in spring training so they would throw it again during the regular season or that he would let one go with the bases empty in the hope of bashing it later with runners on base. Ramírez owned a career average 30 points higher with at least one base occupied. Former major-league pitcher Brian Bannister understood the hitting mastermind that was Manny Ramírez.

"He has such an ambiguous personality," Bannister said. "He doesn't give anything away. You have no idea what he's feeling at the plate. He could be in the middle of a slump or the best hitting streak of his life, and he has that same blank expression on his face. . . . It's freaky. Sometimes,

Sweet-swinging but strange Manny Ramírez shows his form at the plate.
WIKIMEDIA COMMONS

he will just let a pitch go by like he doesn't care. If you're lucky enough to strike him out, he will just kind of walk back to the dugout, like it didn't even matter. And you're on the mound thinking, 'What's going on here? Is he setting me up? What's going on in that head of his?'"[1]

Ramírez was the ultimate anomaly, a mystery wrapped in a riddle. He showed flashes of greatness afield, uncorking an occasional laser to the plate to cut down a runner trying to score or leaping at the ball to make a catch, but his exasperating disinterest and lack of concentration as an outfielder resulted in a career defensive WAR (wins above replacement) of -22.5, which ranks among the worst in baseball history. His brilliance in studying pitchers proved his ability to focus, but every endeavor outside the batter's box screamed the opposite.

The results could be infuriating, hilarious, or both. There was the funny stuff, like when he made a running catch at the wall in Baltimore, high-fived a Red Sox fan in the stands, then fired the ball into the infield to start a double play. Or when he entered the Green Monster to urinate or talk on his cellphone between innings. There was the angering, like when he jogged out grounders or refused to play, citing a mysterious ailment. There were times when the line between frustration and hilarity became blurred, such as when he dove in vain to make a catch, fell, lost his cap, crawled after the ball, rolled over as the ball lodged between his stomach and the grass, and popped up smiling. And there were simply outrageous "Manny Being Manny" moments, such as when he lost his $15,000 diamond earring sliding into third base.

The funny Manny was embraced and the frustrating Manny was endured by fans, teammates, and the Red Sox front office for seven seasons following his arrival in 2001 because the man could simply rake. And it was not a matter of see ball, hit ball. He studied videos of how pitchers he was scheduled to face attacked other hitters. He worked to be great at the plate. "When it comes to his craft, his art, his skill, he's as smart as anyone in the American League," praised fellow superstar Alex Rodriguez. "And he takes it as seriously as anyone in the game."[2]

Much was expected after Ramírez signed an eight-year contract for $160 million and much was delivered. He averaged 36 home runs and 114 RBIs over seven full seasons with the Sox. He led the American

League in on-base percentage three times, in batting average in 2002, and in home runs in 2004, when he earned Most Valuable Player honors in the World Series despite committing what could have been two disastrous errors in Game 1.

Ramírez landed in the center of controversy even as an innocent bystander. The Sox enraged Nomar Garciaparra after the 2003 season when they offered Ramírez to Texas in a proposed deal for superstar shortstop Alex Rodriguez, who landed in New York two months later. But the thick-skinned Ramírez was not one to take such a trade rumor as an affront. The dynamic due of Ramírez and Ortiz combined for a ridiculous 92 homers and 292 RBIs in 2005 as the Red Sox again snagged a wild card berth but lost three straight to Chicago in the first round. Ramírez batted .321 with 35 home runs in just 130 games the following year.

Then came 2007. Ramírez began the season miserably, batting just .202 through April and .244 in late May. He had just eight home runs on June 15. Manny was 35, and it seemed Father Time had finally taken a toll. An oblique strain knocked him out for a month. Manny Being Manny was not so cute when Manny wasn't being Manny at the plate. He did slug two home runs to help the Sox sweep the Angels in the first round of the playoffs, but he shot off his mouth once too often after they lost three of the first four to Cleveland in the American League Championship Series to place themselves on the brink of elimination. "Why should we panic?" he asked. "We have a great team. If it doesn't happen, who cares? There's always next year. It's not like it's the end of the world."[3]

Why couldn't he have just stopped at "We have a great team"? Some took his words as a slap in the face to his teammates, Red Sox Nation, and baseball fans everywhere. Though no game can be considered apocalyptic, many believed Ramírez was scoffing at the passion of the Boston faithful by claiming they were taking the trials and tribulations of their favorite team too seriously. Some in the media criticized Ramírez for what they perceived as flippant comments, but Sox president Larry Lucchino claimed to have interpreted his words otherwise.

"He's just not tight," Lucchino said. "He was trying to say, 'you know, let's don't panic. We're going out and play this game. We're going to have fun'... that's how I took it. I know that certain words there are going to be jumped on, and people are going to suggest other things, but I think what you see in that is the essential Manny Ramírez, and one reason why for seven consecutive years we've seen an exceptional offensive [player]."[4]

He was far from exceptional in 2007, but his drop in production was negated by a 120-RBI season from third baseman Mike Lowell and a pitching staff that ranked atop the American League in team earned run average, thanks greatly to inconsistent 20-game winner Josh Beckett, who put it all together for one year to help the Sox to their first division crown since 1995. The flame-throwing right-hander saved the season in Cleveland by holding the Indians to just one run and striking out 11 in Game 5 to send the series back to Fenway. A sense of doom, which had been following Indians fans for decades, reared its ugly head again as the Sox seemed in control of the series despite still being down. Veteran outfielder J. D. Drew and emerging infield standouts Dustin Pedroia and Kevin Youkilis led a 23-run attack in Games 6 and 7 combined, as back-to-back routs completed the comeback and clinched another pennant for Boston.

That the Red Sox would defeat Colorado in the World Series seemed a foregone conclusion. The surprising Rockies were forced to cool their heels for 10 days after winning the National League Championship Series. They were stale and they played like it. Boston, fresh off its momentum-building return from the dead against the Indians, destroyed its overmatched foe for another World Series sweep. While usual standouts Drew, Lowell, Ortiz, Varitek, Beckett, and Schilling played significant roles in the wipeout, three newer Sox shone bright as well. First baseman Kevin Youkilis, who had moved from third to accommodate Lowell, batted .288 with a .390 on-base percentage that ranked second among the regulars behind only Big Papi. Rookie outfielder Jacoby Ellsbury, who was called up to stay in September and hit safely in 21 of his first 22 games, batted .438 in the series. And 23-year-old southpaw Jon Lester, who had been stricken with blood cancer just a year earlier, blanked the Rockies—in the light air of Coors Field, no less—into the sixth inning to win the clincher.

Lowell could empathize with Lester. The third baseman had been diagnosed with testicular cancer eight years earlier. That gave him a greater thrill as he watched Lester mow down the Rockies. "I'm ecstatic for him," Lowell said. "I don't think too many people expected him to be in that situation and against a very good hitting team in a tough park to pitch in. He did an excellent job. We all know what he's had to overcome and, personally, I feel we have a little bit of a link because of what both of us have gone through."[5]

After securing their second World Series crown in four years following an 86-year drought, the question was no longer if the Red Sox could win a title, but if they could repeat. And, in a lesser light, what baffling stunt would Ramírez pull next and would his desire to leave Boston, which he had been hinting about since 2005, be fulfilled? Arguably the greatest right-handed hitter in Red Sox history, Ramírez was perceived to be more trouble than he was worth by 2008. And that was saying something given that injuries had ravaged the team that season. Ortiz missed 45 games with a torn wrist tendon sheath. Lowell lost time with a torn labrum. Drew sat out months with a bad back.

The Sox needed Ramírez, but the man who had earned a reputation as a good-natured flake had morphed into a malcontent. That dissatisfaction nearly resulted in a trade to the Mets three years earlier. The Sox had had enough after their championship run in 2007 and refused to offer him a contract to keep him around as he approached his free agent year. He managed just 20 home runs and 88 RBIs the previous season, so as his 36th birthday approached, his production no longer overrode the distractions. And the Sox, when healthy, boasted plenty of batting power to overcome his potential absence.

One can speculate that the steroid use to which he admitted had transformed him into an angry young man. He was already irritated over the disrespect from the front office when he engaged in a shoving match with Youkilis in the dugout that was caught on camera. The spat began when Ramírez, who threw a punch at his teammate, complained about the penchant of Youkilis to complain about umpire calls and throw bats and helmets in the dugout after unsatisfying plate appearances. Youkilis had been told by others that such tantrums made him look childish, but Ramírez picked a fight over it. Tempers had already been running high after Youkilis complained that Ramírez did not join his teammates on the field during a brawl earlier in the game until after the bullpens had emptied.

Four weeks later Ramírez picked a fight with Red Sox traveling secretary Jack McCormick. He had requested free tickets for family and friends that McCormick said he could not fulfill. Ramirez shoved the 64-year-old to the ground. Francona arrived and yelled, "What the fuck are you doing?" The manager later told legendary Boston sportswriter Peter Gammons, "Manny Ramírez is the worst human being I've ever met." Francona regretted the remark, but the die had been cast. Ramírez was fined $10,000 and had one foot out the door. He exacerbated the problem by claiming the Red Sox mistreated Hispanics such as Nomar Garciaparra and Pedro Martínez and that they "don't deserve a player like me."[6]

The Sox didn't have him much longer. They dealt him on July 31 to the Dodgers in a three-way deal that netted Pirates outfielder Jason Bay, who racked up career-highs with 36 home runs and 119 RBIs for the Red Sox in 2009 before bolting in free agency. Ramírez tore the cover off the ball for Los Angeles, batting a ridiculous .396 the rest of the 2008 season and earning National League Player of the Month honors in August. But that would prove to be his last hurrah. He bounced around the majors over the next three years under the suspicion of taking performance-enhancing drugs, a truth to which he admitted during an interview with Fox Sports journalist Ken Rosenthal in 2014.

"When you make a mistake in life, no matter what you do, you're going to pay the price," he said. "That's what happened to all of the players that did it. I'm not going to judge people. Everybody is human. Everybody makes mistakes. . . . You're going to feel guilty about what you did. But you did it. You move on. And you learn from it. . . . Sometimes, we get caught up in the moment. We start hanging out with the wrong people."[7]

Manny Being Manny had descended from cute to intolerable during his tumultuous seven-and-a-half seasons in a Boston uniform. But Manny would have been a Hall of Famer had he not joined the PED crowd, and he helped the Red Sox win two world championships. And Sox fans will be forever grateful to him for that.

CHAPTER TWENTY-ONE

Chicken and Championships

IF BOSTON HAD A TOWN CRIER THAT ROAMED THE STREETS BELLOWING the state of its baseball team as August turned to September in 2011, he would have yelled, "It's midnight and all is well!"

That meant status quo. The Red Sox owned a typical 83-52 record and were holding on to first place in the American League East. They were on pace for 100 wins and seemed all but assured of another playoff berth under manager Terry Francona, who had guided the team to the brink of the World Series in 2008 and again into the postseason in 2009. More than three millions fans had streamed into Fenway Park to watch their beloved bashers lead all of baseball in runs scored.

The key cast of characters had changed little since the title run of 2007. Mike Lowell had been replaced in the lineup by former Padres first baseman Adrián González, who was in the process of compiling a career-best .338 batting average, leading the league with 213 hits and driving in 117 runs. Outfield addition speedster Carl Crawford was fading. But Dustin Pedroia, Kevin Youkilis, Jacoby Ellsbury, J. D. Drew, and David Ortiz still terrorized opposing pitchers in Red Sox uniforms. Josh Beckett, Jon Lester, and Tim Wakefield remained in the starting rotation, and closer Jonathan Papelbon had stayed steady as one of the premier closers in the sport. The bunch that had captured a crown four years earlier indeed appeared destined to play for another one.

But that fictional town crier would have had quite a different message a month later. The Sox shockingly experienced one of the most epic collapses in baseball history—both on the field and in the clubhouse.

They dropped two straight to start September and permanently fall out of first place. The Sox remained nine games ahead of Tampa Bay for a wild card spot, however, which seemed assured. They lost six of seven on a road trip that included a three-game sweep to the Rays that chopped their advantage to 3½ games. They dropped three of four at home to Tampa Bay a week later as their lead shrunk to two. Defeats in five of their next six games all but wiped it out. And when the Rays won their last five while Boston went 2-3, it was over. The Red Sox were on vacation.

The blame on the field could not be placed on the hitters. They scored in double figures five times in September and averaged 5.4 runs per game. The guilt lay squarely upon the likes of Beckett, Lester, Wakefield, and fellow starter John Lackey. The quartet sported a record of 3-9 that month while allowing 71 runs in 102⅓ innings for a combined earned run average of 6.19. Lackey was the worst offender. He surrendered 24 runs in 23⅔ innings. The veteran right-hander had remained in the rotation by reputation alone. His season-ending ERA of 6.41 was easily the worst of his career.

That was only part of the starters' problem. A perception developed that they did not care about their struggles or that of the team. Media

Budding superstar Mookie Betts shows the MVP form of 2018.
WIKIMEDIA COMMONS

reports emerged that Beckett, Lester, and Lackey spent much of their time when not on the mound during games drinking beer, eating fast-food fried chicken, and playing video games in the clubhouse. They were charged with disloyalty to teammates battling for a playoff spot. A soap opera had developed in which one of the main characters was Francona, who some felt had grown distracted by a marriage problem that forced him to live in a hotel room during the season. The manager insisted after the dreams of a postseason died that, though he had lost influence on some veteran players, his mind had been on baseball.

"It makes me angry that people say these things because I've busted my [butt] to be the best manager I can be," he said. "I wasn't terribly successful this year, but I worked harder and spent more time at the ballpark this year than I ever did."[1]

Francona would not spend time at Fenway again until he arrived as a visiting manager of the Cleveland Indians. Despite having led the Red Sox to their first two World Series titles since 1918, he was fired immediately after the season and replaced by Bobby Valentine, who had not managed a major-league team in a decade. A seething Francona bided his time before co-authoring a book with *Boston Globe* columnist Dan Shaughnessy titled *Francona: The Red Sox Years*, in which he lambasted team ownership for perceived meddling in his job duties, obsessing over television ratings, and fostering an unhealthy desire to land more so-called star players on the roster at the expense of performance. The authors crafted the following in railing against Red Sox ownership.

Our owners in Boston, they've been owners for 10 years. They come in with all these ideas about baseball, but I don't think they love baseball. I think they like baseball. It's revenue, and I know that's their right and their interest because they're owners—and they're good owners. But they don't love the game. It's still more of a toy or a hobby for them. It's not their blood. They're going to come in and out of baseball. It's different for me. Baseball is my life.[2]

Francona got on with his life by turning around the Indians while Red Sox management got on with their lives by tinkering with the roster and hoping the 2011 collapse would prove to be an anomaly. It did not. At least that's what new general manager Ben Cherington indicated on August 25, 2012. With his team barely over .500 but on the periphery of the playoff race, he blew up the roster, trading Beckett, González, and Crawford to the Dodgers for five cheap nobodies that remained nobodies. Beckett was on the downside of his usual good-year, bad-year run, Crawford lost time to an elbow injury and hated playing in Boston, and Valentine believed González was devoid of passion and leadership. The deal shed $260 million in salary, giving the franchise future financial flexibility.

A week later, with Boston amid a six-game losing streak that all but destroyed any postseason hopes, Valentine reacted angrily to sports talk host Glenn Ordway when asked in an on-air telephone interview if he had given up on the season. "What an embarrassing thing to say," Valentine began. "If I were there right now, I'd punch you right in the mouth."[3]

The manager later claimed he was joking, but the incident just added to the misery that proved to be the team's worst season since 1965. Cherington continued to hope the standouts that remained in the lineup and rotation would revert to form. He fired Valentine and hired Francona friend John Farrell as manager in 2013.

And indeed, the magic returned. Ortiz, who had lost half of the previous season to injury, paced an attack along with Pedroia and new first baseman and free agent acquisition Mike Napoli that scored 119 more runs than it had in 2012 to lead the American League. Lester and Lackey, who had lost the previous year to Tommy John surgery, rebounded to perform well on the mound while previously inconsistent Clay Buchholz embarked on a stunning stretch of dominance, winning 12 of 13 decisions, posting a 1.74 ERA, and landing on the All-Star team. Buchholz lost three months to a neck injury but picked up right where he left off in September to help the Sox clinch the American League East crown.

And unlike the September disaster that destroyed the 2011 team, this bunch played its best baseball with the division title hanging in the balance. A 21-21 stretch in July and August placed them in a tie for the top with 31 games remaining in the regular season. But the Sox ran away

A smiling John Farrell guided the Red Sox to a World Series title.
WIKIMEDIA COMMONS

and hid with a 17-4 tear that catapulted them nearly 10 games ahead in mid-September.

Fans in Boston, however, had not been judging their team by regular-season success since the Impossible Dream of 1967 launched the Sox into the stratosphere of major-league franchises. They would have to prove their greatness in the playoffs—and they did just that. Brilliant performances by Ellsbury and Ortiz, as well as Lester and fellow starter

Scrappy second baseman Dustin Pedroia taking practice before a game in 2016.
WIKIMEDIA COMMONS

Jake Peavy, pushed them past the Rays in the division series. Then Lester, Lackey, and lights-out closer Koji Uehara shut down the Tigers to send Boston into another clash for the crown against St. Louis.

What happened next cemented Ortiz as a Sox legend and gave him a status along with Yastrzemski as the most clutch player and arguably the most popular in franchise history (given the boos that rained down upon Ted Williams at Fenway Park). Big Papi hit a two-run homer in Game 1 to back the shutout pitching of Lester. He homered again the next night and went 3-for-3 in Game 4 as Buchholz and the bullpen crew shut down St. Louis to tie the series at 2–2. Ortiz again slammed three hits to aid a Lester victory, then clinched the third World Series title in 10 years with four walks and two runs in Game 6. Three of those free passes were intentional as the Cardinals had grown understandably leery of pitching to him. It was among the greatest Fall Classic performances ever. When the last pitch had been thrown and the champagne had stopped flowing, Ortiz owned a ridiculous .688 batting average, equally absurd .760 on-base percentage, and a World Series MVP.

Farrell certainly deserved credit as well. He had assuredly guided what had been a ship on stormy seas a year earlier through a calm journey. The team had brightened an entire city that had been devastated by the bombing attack at the Boston Marathon early in the season. *Boston Globe* columnist Dan Shaughnessy touched upon that in his piece after the ultimate triumph, comparing the togetherness of Farrell and his players positively to that of past Red Sox teams and writing the following:

> *Bottom line: After the death and disruption of mid-April, the 2013 Sox made most everyone around here feel good again. The Sox were likeable, and more important, they liked one another. A franchise famous for "25 guys, 25 cabs" became a magic bus of harmony, team-work, and camaraderie. These highly paid, professional ballplayers actually enjoyed playing baseball and ignored the white noise that is so much a part of the Boston baseball experience.*[4]

Shaughnessy could have copied and pasted that column and saved it for 2018, changing only the names and a few details. The Boston bunch that year also fit like a hand and glove. But much had changed leading up to the fourth World Series championship since 2004, not the least of which was the retirement of Ortiz—mercifully for opposing pitchers. Big Papi finished with a flourish. Unlike most stars that lose their twinkle as they fade into the sunset, he saved arguably his best for last in 2016, batting .315 and leading the American League with 127 RBIs while smashing 38 home runs and a career-high 48 doubles.

Ortiz had helped the Sox rebound from two losing seasons and return to the playoffs that year. And after Cleveland completed a three-

Arm-whipping southpaw Chris Sale helped the Red Sox win it all in 2018.
WIKIMEDIA COMMONS

game division series sweep at Fenway, the fans who cherished him did not merely shuffle to the exits. They chanted "We're not leaving" and "Thank you, Papi" until he emerged from the dugout. Ortiz, always the class act, allowed the Indians to complete their celebration before walking to the mound to wave goodbye and shed a few tears. He waxed philosophic when it was all over.

"The game, the game I love, the game that made me who I am," he said. "The game that I look forward to [getting] better every day is something that I'm definitely going to carry for the rest of my life. And those moments, they're always going to be special. They're always going to stay with you."[5]

The swan song for Ortiz launched a new era of Boston baseball. Just as Carl Yastrzemski had replaced Ted Williams at the plate and in the hearts and minds of Red Sox fans more than a half-century earlier, a new superstar emerged to replace Big Papi. And that was outfielder Mookie Betts, who broke through in 2016 by batting .313 with 31 home runs and 113 RBIs and leading the league with 129 runs to place second in the Most Valuable Player voting. Meanwhile, the mound trio of Cy Young Award winner Rick Porcello, veteran lefty David Price, and shut-down closer Craig Kimbrel provided hope after a 2015 season in which the Red Sox ranked a woeful 14th in team ERA.

President of baseball operations Dave Dombrowski continued to infuse the team with top talent new and old. Young Xander Bogaerts had emerged as one of the premier shortstops in the game. Brilliant rookie outfielder Andrew Benintendi arrived in 2017 to drive in 90 runs and place second in the Rookie of the Year balloting. Southpaw sidearm slinger Chris Sale was swapped from the White Sox that season to sport a 17-9 record and strike out a whopping 308, five short of the franchise record set by Pedro Martínez in 1999.

Yet despite the brilliance on the field, the Sox could not put it all together to dominate the regular season or embark on a long playoff run. That is, until Farrell was gone and they played under new manager Alex Cora in 2018. The Sox opened their checkbook in the offseason to sign slugging outfielder J. D. Martinez, who nearly won the MVP after hitting .302 with 43 home runs and a league-high 130 RBIs. The honor instead went to Betts, who won the batting title at .346 and paced the junior circuit with 129 runs. That devastating pair combined with Bogaerts and Benintendi to pace an attack that led the American League in runs scored. Meanwhile, Sale and Kimbrel headlined a pitching staff that boasted enough depth to help Boston set a franchise record with 108 wins and run away with the Eastern Division title. The Red Sox had not won two consecutive regular-season crowns for more than a century—

now they had three straight. And they set out to prove their historic greatness in the playoffs.

The first step was a doozy—a division series battle against the 100-win Bronx Bombers, who had lived up to their nickname in 2018 by mashing 267 home runs. But times had changed. The Curse had long been slain. The Yankees now served as the punching bag for the Sox, who dispatched them in four games and held them to just 14 total runs. Included was a 16–1 slaughter at Yankee Stadium in Game 3 in which every Boston starter hit safely.

The next victim was defending World Series champion Houston, which was dispatched with equal ease. Among the heroes was Price, who exorcised demons that had resulted in a 1-9 postseason record as a starter by pitching six shutout innings with nine strikeouts in Game 5 to beat Astros ace Justin Verlander and catapult the Sox into a World Series showdown against the Dodgers. An opening-game defeat to Houston had been followed by four consecutive victories.

That was no monkey lifted off the back of Price—it was a gorilla. Freed from the stigma of playoff failures, the left-hander keyed a blitz of Los Angeles with two more triumphs. He gave Boston a 2–0 lead by holding the hard-hitting Dodgers to just two runs in six innings, then clinched the championship with a tremendous seven-inning perfor-mance in Game 5 aided by an out-of-nowhere two-homer explosion by unlikely hero Steve Pearce.

The World Series victory that followed a 108-win regular season and dominant American League playoff blitz cemented the 2018 Red Sox as one of the greatest teams in baseball history. "When you say that, it's almost overwhelming, because you just never think that you'll be associated with a club that can do that—you talk about 119-57, those numbers are mind-boggling," said Dombrowski. "You think you have a good club, you might win 105 or something with the postseason and you're really satisfied. But you start talking about it, it's winning more than two-thirds of your games over the year, so no, I don't think you can really grasp it. I think it's a tribute to all these guys, because you don't get to that point unless you're talented and also you grind, you really work through things, you bounce back, you're resilient and you're tough, and that's this group."[6]

Indeed, the Boston Red Sox had earned their status as the most dominant franchise of the young century. And there was nothing to indicate that standing in Major League Baseball would change anytime soon.

Chapter Twenty-Two

Red Sox Nation

RED SOX NATION IS THE OFFICIAL TEAM FAN CLUB. BUT IT REPRESENTS far more than that. It is a far-flung fandom with followers throughout the world. It is a passion captured in movie and song. It is tradition. It is the agony and the ecstasy, as played out after galling defeats to the hated Yankees and World Series victory parades that attract millions.

The term was coined by *Boston Globe* feature writer Nathan Cobb during the 1986 Red Sox–Mets battle for the crown. His article spotlighted the divide between fans of the two teams in the southwestern Connecticut town of Milford. Cobb wrote nearly two decades later of his unawareness of his place in Red Sox lore and assumption that legendary *Globe* compatriot Dan Shaughnessy was the founding father of Red Sox Nation. Indeed, Shaughnessy coined "Curse of the Bambino" with his 1990 book of the same name. But it was Cobb that launched Red Sox Nation.

Not that an unnamed Red Sox Nation didn't exist previously. Hardcore fans of the team could be found throughout the upper northeast United States. Transplants that wear their Sox fandom on their sleeves are scattered around the country and beyond. For generations they were tied together not only by their love of the Red Sox but also a passionate hatred for the players in pinstripes. One fan quoted in a 2013 book titled *Rooting for the Home Team* offered years before the cathartic four-title run after the turn of the century, "It's bad enough we haven't won since 1918. It's worse that [the Yankees] have won twenty-six times since then. Much worse. It's New York. Goddamned New York." It is the diversity of emotion experienced by Boston fans that inspired former Red Sox pitcher Dennis Eckersley to assert that the franchise boasts "the most manic-depressive fan base."[1]

That fan base has embraced traditions unlike those of any other team. One of them revolves around the 1969 Neil Diamond hit "Sweet Caroline." The tune that boasted no previous ties to Boston, Fenway Park, or the Red Sox became connected to all three in 1997, when team employee Amy Tobey, who was in charge of music selection at the ballpark and had noted its popularity at other sports venues, began playing it between the seventh and ninth innings of games. The positive reaction from fans motivated Tobey to play it more often, particularly when the Sox were winning and her gut instinct told her they were going to close it out. "I actually considered it like a good luck charm," she said. "Even if they were just one run [ahead], I might still do it. It was just a feel."[2]

New Red Sox management in 2002 took it a step beyond, insisting that Tobey play "Sweet Caroline" in the eighth inning of every game. The superstitious among Boston fans might claim that the tradition helped their team break the Curse of the Bambino two years later. No matter—singing it at the ballpark has evolved into a beloved ritual.

1960s band The Standells, whose hit "Dirty Water" championed the city of Boston and became a fan favorite.

The Diamond classic is not the only song associated with the Red Sox. Another is the 1966 one-hit wonder by a Los Angeles rock band called the Standells titled "Dirty Water," which is a tribute to the Charles River. Oddly, none of its members had even been to Boston or seen the Charles River when the song was produced. But band producer Ed Cobb had just visited and was inspired to write it. "Dirty Water" has followed a similar path as "Sweet Caroline." Both began to be played at Fenway in 1997. But while the latter is played during hopeful Red Sox victories, the former blares from the loudspeakers after a triumph has been assured.

A band more associated with modern Red Sox baseball are the punk-rocking and politically active Dropkick Murphys, who were born and raised in nearby Quincy. The group gained an association with the team through its 2004 hit "Tessie," which was used in the movie *Fever Pitch*, starring Jimmy Fallon, who played an incurably passionate Red Sox fan. The Dropkick Murphys played the song at the premiere of the film, which was held at Fenway Park. The band also played at the 2007, 2013, and 2018 World Series championship parades.

Neil Diamond sings adopted Red Sox fans song "Sweet Caroline" during a nationally televised July 4 event in 2009.
WIKIMEDIA COMMONS

A far more distant and important tradition tied to the franchise is the Jimmy Fund for cancer care and research, which can be traced back to 1948. The charity initially launched through a national radio broadcast, and in which the National League Boston Braves (which won the pennant that year) participated, was left without an area team when that club moved to Milwaukee in 1953. The Red Sox picked up the baton and has been running with it ever since.

Owner Tom Yawkey and superstar Ted Williams, who had been involved for years, spearheaded franchise involvement in the money-raising venture through various creative ideas. Among the earliest was the Jimmy Fund Contribution Ball; fans dropped donations into slots while voting for their favorite Red Sox player. Players visited cancer-stricken children at the Jimmy Fund Clinic. Veteran play-by-play broadcaster Ken Coleman later served as the charity's executive director.

Support for the Jimmy Fund evolved in a variety of spotlighting initiatives, such as the massive sign that served as the only billboard in Fenway Park for a half-century. Yawkey made certain that the charity was mentioned and promoted in each Red Sox broadcast. Among the players that furthered the tradition was Carl Yastrzemski, whose efforts led to a full $5,000 share of the 1967 World Series winnings being donated to the Jimmy Fund. New ownership in 2002 did not slow the train. Fiftieth and sixtieth anniversary celebrations of the franchise partnership with the charity were held in 2003 and 2013, respectively.

But songs, movies, and charities could never define Red Sox Nation. They could never nail down fan passion. Red Sox Nation is not a number of people. Red Sox fandom is not the folks that visit Fenway a few times a year and watch the team on TV. It is the feeling of frustration of those around the world who lived and died during an 86-year title drought. It is the unbridled joy of those around the globe who experienced the cathartic euphoria of 2004, some of whom traveled thousands of miles to join the celebration. They are the lovers of the Splendid Splinter, Yaz, Youk, and Big Papi. They are inextricably tied to Red Sox history good and bad. And they will remain fervent fans forever.

Notes

Chapter 1: Super Cy and the First Series Champs

1. Steph Diorio, "Red Sox History: The Huntington Avenue Grounds, As Seen by Nuf Ced," SB Nation: Over the Monster, April 1, 2016, https://www.overthemonster.com/2016/4/1/11344478/red-sox-history-huntington-avenue-grounds-tessie.
2. Ibid.
3. Peter Golenbock, *Red Sox Nation: The Rich and Colorful History of the Boston Red Sox* (Chicago: Triumph Books, 2015), 22.
4. Bill Nowlin and David Southwick, "Cy Young," Society for American Baseball Research, https://sabr.org/bioproj/person/dae2fb8a.
5. Ibid.
6. National Baseball Hall of Fame, Cy Young, https://baseballhall.org/hall-of-famers/young-cy.
7. Cy Young, Baseball Reference, https://www.baseball-reference.com/players/y/youngcy01.shtml.
8. Nowlin and Southwick, "Cy Young."
9. Trevor Hammond, "Baseball's First World Series: October 1-13, 1903," Fish Wrap, October 1, 2016, https://blog.newspapers.com/baseballs-first-world-series-october-1-13-1903/.
10. This Great Game, "1903: The First World Series," www.thisgreatgame.com/1903-baseball-history.html.
11. Diorio, "Red Sox History."
12. Tony Pettinato, "Boston Defeats Pittsburgh in Baseball's First World Series," Genealogy Bank, October 13, 2016, https://blog.genealogybank.com/boston-defeats-pittsburgh-in-baseballs-first-world-series.html.

Chapter 2: Fenway and the *Monstah*

1. Peter Golenbock, *Red Sox Nation: The Rich and Colorful History of the Boston Red Sox* (Chicago: Triumph Books, 2015), 28.
2. Ibid., 30.
3. Hayden Bird, "The Green Monster Emerged from the Ashes of Fenway Fires," Boston.com, July 17, 2016, https://www.boston.com/sports/boston-red-sox/2016/07/17/fenway-fires.
4. Golenbock, *Red Sox Nation*, 31.

5. Saul Wisnia, "Fenway Park's First Day in 1912: Peanuts, the Titanic and the Boston Red Sox," Bleacher Report, April 20, 2012, https://bleacherreport.com/articles/1153029 -fenway-parks-first-day-in-1912-peanuts-the-titanic-and-the-red-sox.

6. Bird, "The Green Monster Emerged."

7. Ibid.

8. Jimmy Golen, "At Fenway, Sitting on Top of the World," *Washington Post*, April 6, 2003, https://www.washingtonpost.com/archive/sports/2003/04/06/at-fenway-sitting-on -top-of-the-world/5549c1df-3f7d-4b1a-811e-a6c8eae19fbe/?utm_term=.6395c41412f6.

9. Red Sox Diehard, "What Makes Fenway Fenway?", www.redsoxdiehard.com/ fenway/unique.html.

10. David Kagan, "The Physics of Pesky's Pole," Hardball Times, October 22, 2014, https://tht.fangraphs.com/the-physics-of-peskys-pole/.

11. Red Sox Diehard, "What Makes Fenway Fenway?"

Chapter 3: The Annual Champs

1. Peter Golenbock, *Red Sox Nation: The Rich and Colorful History of the Boston Red Sox* (Chicago: Triumph Books, 2015), 35.

2. Lew Freedman, *The 50 Greatest Players in Boston Red Sox History* (Philadelphia: Camino Books, 2013).

3. Golenbock, *Red Sox Nation*, 46–47.

4. Freedman, *50 Greatest Players*, 61.

5. Cliff Corcoran, "99 Cool Facts About Babe Ruth," *Sports Illustrated*, July 11, 2013, https://www.si.com/mlb/strike-zone/2013/07/12/99-cool-facts-about-babe-ruth.

6. Golenbock, *Red Sox Nation*, 57.

Chapter 4: Creating the Curse

1. Martin Gitlin, *Powerful Moments in Sports: The Most Significant Sporting Events in American History* (Lanham, MD: Rowman and Littlefield, 2017), 14.

2. Ibid., 15.

3. Larry Getlen, "The Real Reason the Sox Sold Babe Ruth," *New York Post*, March 6, 2016, https://nypost.com/2016/03/06/the-real-reason-the-red-sox-sold-babe-ruth/.

4. Curt Smith, *The Red Sox Fan's Little Book of Wisdom: A Fine Sense of the Ridiculous* (Boulder, CO: Taylor Trade Publishing, 2002), https://books.google.com/ books?id=WeYlAAAAQBAJ&pg=PT16&lpg=PT16&dq=%22They%27re+the+only +friends+that+SOB+has:+Harry+Frazee+My+Lady+Friends&source=bl&ots=u5Ww 5TqTns&sig=ACfU3U3W_Y0YovA2G4dpUuyTyhNEKFD6BQ&hl=en&sa=X&ved =2ahUKEwizkJiS55rgAhWQ3oMKHTcACwQQ6AEwAHoECAkQAQ#v=onepage &q=%22They're%20the%20only%20friends%20that%20SOB%20has%3A%20Harry %20Frazee%20My%20Lady%20.

5. James C. O'Leary, "Red Sox Sell Babe Ruth for $100,000 Cash," Boston Globe, January 6, 1920, https://www.bostonglobe.com/sports/1920/01/06/red-sox-sell-babe -ruth-for-cash/muYGoMdAzCl8WlRHK2LumI/story.html.

6. Gitlin, *Powerful Moments in Sports*, 17.

7. Peter Golenbock. *Red Sox Nation: The Rich and Colorful History of the Boston Red Sox* (Chicago: Triumph Books, 2015), 62.

CHAPTER 5: THE MORASS

1. Peter Golenbock, *Red Sox Nation: The Rich and Colorful History of the Boston Red Sox* (Chicago: Triumph Books, 2015), 63.
2. New England Historical Society, "Sunday Baseball Fails to Rescue the Boston Red Sox from the Cellar in 1929," www.newenglandhistoricalsociety.com/sunday-baseball-fails-to-rescue-the-boston-red-sox-from-the-cellar-in-1929/.
3. Golenbock, *Red Sox Nation*, 66.
4. Ibid., 71.
5. Ibid., 72.
6. Dave Heller, "The Tragic Death of 'Big Ed' Morris," Seamheads.com, September 21, 2010, http://seamheads.com/blog/2010/09/21/the-tragic-death-of-big-ed-morris/.
7. New England Historical Society, "Sunday Baseball."

CHAPTER 6: THE YAWKEY WAY

1. Al Hirshberg, *The Red Sox, The Bean and the Cod* (New York: Waverly House, 1947), 15–17.
2. National Baseball Hall of Fame, "Tom Yawkey," https://baseballhall.org/hall-of-famers/yawkey-tom.
3. Mark R. Millikin, *Jimmie Foxx: The Pride of Sudlersville* (Lanham, MD: The Scarecrow Press, 1998), 180–81, https://books.google.com/books?id=OLdQwc3uXu4C&pg=PA180&lpg=PA180&dq=How+did+the+Red+Sox+rip+off+Athletics+for+Jimmie+Foxx?&source=bl&ots=WYoafqFVjI&sig=ACfU3U2OLNuPpjaGiblh2mBq9jItfDtndg&hl=en&sa=X&ved=2ahUKEwiumO736J_gAhVl4YMKHVLABF8Q6AEwDHoECAIQAQ#v=onepage&q=How%20did%20the%20Red%20Sox%20rip%20off%20Athletics%20for%20Jimmie%20Foxx%3F&f=false.
4. Mark Armour, "Tom Yawkey," Society for American Baseball Research, https://sabr.org/bioproj/person/6382f9d5.
5. Peter Golenbock, *Red Sox Nation: The Rich and Colorful History of the Boston Red Sox* (Chicago: Triumph Books, 2015), 93.

CHAPTER 7: THE GROWTH OF THE SPLENDID SPLINTER

1. Samantha Burkett, "Ted Williams Made Big League Debut in Front of 11 Hall of Famers," National Baseball Hall of Fame, https://baseballhall.org/discover/short-stops/ted-williams-mlb-debut.
2. Josh Jackson, "Williams, Padres Gave San Diego Thrill in 30s," MiLB.com, March 13, 2017, https://www.milb.com/milb/news/boston-red-sox-legend-ted-williams-was-a-rookie-with-hometown-san-diego-padres-in-pacific-coast-league/c-215058460.
3. Ibid.
4. Peter Golenbock, *Red Sox Nation: The Rich and Colorful History of the Boston Red Sox* (Chicago: Triumph Books, 2015), 115.

5. Dick Hackenberg, "'I Wanted to Crash Majors. But I'm Not Ready Yet!' Says Ted Williams," *Minneapolis Star*, March 29, 1938, https://www.newspapers.com/clip/26623088/1938_ted_williams_not_ready_for_the/.

6. John F. Kennedy Presidential Library and Museum, "The Immortal Life of Ted Williams," December 8, 2013, https://www.jfklibrary.org/events-and-awards/forums/past-forums/transcripts/the-immortal-life-of-ted-williams.

7. Bill Nowlin, Ted Williams, Society for American Baseball Research, https://sabr.org/bioproj/person/35baa190.

8. Bill Pennington, "Ted Williams's .406 Is More Than a Number," *New York Times*, September 17, 2011, https://www.nytimes.com/2011/09/18/sports/baseball/ted-williamss-406-average-is-more-than-a-number.html.

9. Ibid.

Chapter 8: The Championship, the Choice, and the Choke

1. Newspaper Alum, "Cardinals vs. Red Sox Epic 7-Game Clashes: 1946 and 1947," https://www.newspaperalum.com/2013/10/cardinals-vs-red-sox-epic-7-game-clashes-1946-and-1967.html.

2. Peter Golenbock, *Red Sox Nation: The Rich and Colorful History of the Boston Red Sox* (Chicago: Triumph Books, 2015), 164.

3. Terry Sloope, Rudy York, Society for American Baseball Research, https://sabr.org/bioproj/person/e31f1169.

4. Golenbock, *Red Sox Nation*, 169–70.

5. Gordon Edes, "Red October—Oct. 5, 1948—The Curious Tale of Denny Galehouse," Medium.com, October 7, 2018, https://medium.com/@gewrite/red-october-oct-5-1948-the-curious-tale-of-denny-galehouse-c5eeb224b56b.

6. Golenbock, *Red Sox Nation*, 183.

Chapter 9: Pushing for Pumpsie

1. Connor Dolan, "The Significance of Changing Yawkey Way," First and Fan, May 4, 2018, http://firstandfan.com/2018/05/the-significance-of-changing-yawkey-way/.

2. Ibid.

3. Ibid.

4. Peter Golenbock, *Red Sox Nation: The Rich and Colorful History of the Boston Red Sox* (Chicago: Triumph Books, 2015), 226.

5. John Shea and Scott Ostler, "Pumpsie Green, Who Integrated Red Sox, Opens Up About Trail-Blazing Career," *San Francisco Chronicle*, October 27, 2018, https://www.sfchronicle.com/giants/shea/article/Pumpsie-Green-The-baseball-trailblazer-who-13340020.php.

6. Bill Nowlin, "Pumpsie Green," Society for American Baseball Research, https://sabr.org/bioproj/person/f9472d8a.

7. New England Historical Society, "Pumpsie Green Gets a Standing O for Breaking the Color Barrier," www.newenglandhistoricalsociety.com/pumpsie-green-gets-standing-o-breaking-color-barrier/.

CHAPTER 10: YAZ AND THE IMPOSSIBLE DREAM

1. Baseball Almanac, "Carl Yastrzemski Quotes," www.baseball-almanac.com/quotes/quoyaz.shtml.
2. Peter Golenbock, *Red Sox Nation: The Rich and Colorful History of the Boston Red Sox* (Chicago: Triumph Books, 2015), 289–90.
3. *Hartford Courant*, "From the Pages of *Ball Four*," July 26, 1998, https://www.courant.com/news/connecticut/hc-xpm-1998-07-26-9807260183-story.html.
4. Bill Nowlin, "1967 Red Sox: Spring Training," Society for American Baseball Research, https://sabr.org/research/1967-red-sox-spring-training.
5. Greg Sullivan, "The 1967 Red Sox Part 2—'It's Pandemonium on the Field,'" *Oak Ridger*, September 28, 2007, https://www.oakridger.com/x775334736.
6. Ibid.
7. Bud Collins, "Again—Our Phoenix Rises: Just Plain Witchcraft," *Boston Globe*, October 12, 1967, passage excerpted: https://sabr.org/gamesproj/game/october-12-1967-gibson-cardinals-lift-cardinals-title-over-impossible-dream-red-sox.
8. Associated Press, "Red Sox Knocking on Destiny's Door," *New York Times*, October 12, 1967, passage excerpted: https://sabr.org/gamesproj/game/october-12-1967-gibson-cardinals-lift-cardinals-title-over-impossible-dream-red-sox.
9. Bud Collins, "Sweet Memories Will Follow Sadness," *Boston Globe*, October 13, 1967, https://www.bostonglobe.com/sports/1967/10/13/sweet-memories-will-follow-sadness-red-sox-loss/LmPWtqyFfTSwHIuhS2j4JJ/story.html.

CHAPTER 11: THE TRAGIC TALE OF TONY C.

1. Bill Nowlin, "Tony Conigliaro," Society for American Baseball Research, https://sabr.org/bioproj/person/52ad9113.
2. Ibid.
3. YouTube, "Tony Conigliaro—Playing the Field," posted August 26, 2010, https://www.youtube.com/watch?v=p5whptzs1g8.
4. Don Amore, "After Tony C Was Hit," *Hartford Courant*, August 18, 1992, https://www.courant.com/news/connecticut/hc-xpm-1992-08-18-0000113585-story.html.
5. Lew Freedman, *The 50 Greatest Players in Boston Red Sox History* (Philadelphia: Camino Books, 2013), 122.
6. Peter Golenbock, *Red Sox Nation: The Rich and Colorful History of the Boston Red Sox* (Chicago: Triumph Books, 2015), 337.
7. Freedman, *50 Greatest Players*, 123.

CHAPTER 12: A GREAT PAIR OF NEW SOX

1. Tom Nahigian, Fred Lynn, Society for American Baseball Research, https://sabr.org/bioproj/person/7fb674d5.
2. Neil Keefe, "Transcript: Jim Rice's Hall of Fame Induction Speech," NESN, July 26, 2009, https://nesn.com/2009/07/transcript-jim-rices-hall-of-fame-induction-speech/.
3. *Miami News*, "Rice Riled Over Quote in Mag," June 22, 1978, https://newspaperarchive.com/miami-news-record-jun-22-1978-p-6/.

4. Greg Sullivan, "1975 Red Sox Revisited: Hawk Harrelson's Return to Boston," *Herald News*, May 1, 2015, https://www.heraldnews.com/article/20150417/SPORTS/150416270.

5. Fox Sports, "1975 World Series: An Eyewitness History," October 28, 2015, https://www.foxsports.com/mlb/just-a-bit-outside/story/cincinnati-reds-boston-red-sox-1975-world-series-pete-rose-carlton-fisk-oral-history-102815.

6. Doug Wilson, *Pudge: The Biography of Carlton Fisk* (New York: St. Martin's Press, 2015), 129, https://books.google.com/books?id=-f65BwAAQBAJ&pg=PA129&lpg=PA129&dq=Google+books#v=onepage&q&f=false.

7. Fox Sports, "1975 World Series: An Eyewitness History."

8. Scott Tinley, "Glory Days of the *Boston Globe*: The Greatest Sports Staff Ever," *Sports Illustrated*, June 3, 2009, https://www.si.com/more-sports/2009/06/03/globe.

9. Curry Kirkpatrick, "In an Orbit All His Own," *Sports Illustrated*, August 7, 1978, https://www.si.com/vault/1978/08/07/822849/in-an-orbit-all-his-own-bill-lee-the-spaceman-takes-a-different-track-whether-hes-quotretiringquot-from-the-red-sox-lofting-a-leephus-pitch-or-probing-the-wisdom-of-zevon.

10. Fox Sports, "1975 World Series: An Eyewitness History."

Chapter 13: The So-Called Spaceman

1. Curry Kirkpatrick, "In an Orbit All His Own," *Sports Illustrated*, August 7, 1978, https://www.si.com/vault/1978/08/07/822849/in-an-orbit-all-his-own-bill-lee-the-spaceman-takes-a-different-track-whether-hes-quotretiringquot-from-the-red-sox-lofting-a-leephus-pitch-or-probing-the-wisdom-of-zevon.

2. Ibid.

3. Lew Freedman, *The 50 Greatest Players in Boston Red Sox History* (Philadelphia: Camino Books, 2013), 143.

4. Peter Golenbock, *Red Sox Nation: The Rich and Colorful History of the Boston Red Sox* (Chicago: Triumph Books, 2015), 395–96.

5. Jim Prime, "Bill Lee," Society for American Baseball Research, https://sabr.org/bioproj/person/ac80db85.

Chapter 14: Bucky Freaking Dent and the Pain of '78

1. Dan Epstein, *Big Hair and Plastic Grass: A Funky Ride Through Baseball and America in the Swinging 70s* (New York: St. Martin's Press, 2010), 213–14.

2. Peter Gammons, "The Boston Massacre," *Sports Illustrated*, September 17, 1978, https://www.si.com/vault/issue/70795/31.

3. Joseph Wancho, "October 1, 1978: Cleveland's Rick Waits Handcuffs Yankees, Forces Playoff with Red Sox for AL East Title," Society for American Baseball Research, https://sabr.org/gamesproj/game/october-1-1978-clevelands-rick-waits-handcuffs-yankees-forces-playoff-red-sox-al-east.

4. "A Day of Light and Shadows," WNYC, February 4, 2014, https://www.wnyc.org/story/day-light-and-shadows/.

5. Ibid.

6. Peter Gammons, "There's Life After Death," *Sports Illustrated*, October 8, 1978, https://www.si.com/vault/issue/70801/33.

Chapter 15: Rocket Roger

1. Frederick C. Bush, Roger Clemens, Society for American Baseball Research, https://sabr.org/bioproj/person/b5a2be2f.
2. Ibid.
3. Alan Schwarz, "What Scouts Said . . . ," ESPN, June 2, 2004, www.espn.com/mlb/columns/story?columnist=schwarz_alan&id=1813664.
4. Kevin Dupont, "Yastrzemski Bids a Fond Farewell," *New York Times*, October 2, 1983, https://www.nytimes.com/1983/10/02/sports/yastrzemski-bids-a-fond-farewell.html.
5. Lew Freedman, *The 50 Greatest Players in Boston Red Sox History* (Philadelphia: Camino Books, 2013), 39–40.
6. Peter Golenbock, *Red Sox Nation: The Rich and Colorful History of the Boston Red Sox* (Chicago: Triumph Books, 2015), 416.
7. Paul Doyle, "Clemens Throws a Curve," *Hartford Courant*, December 14, 1996, https://www.courant.com/news/connecticut/hc-xpm-1996-12-14-9612140364-story.html.

Chapter 16: Buckner's Boo-Boo

1. Bruce Markusen, "Cooperstown Confidential: The Sad Saga of Oil Can Boyd," Hardball Times, May 4, 2012, https://tht.fangraphs.com/cooperstown-confidential-the-sad-saga-of-oil-can-boyd1/.
2. Ross Newhan, "A Seaver vs. Sutton Showdown Goes Down with Seaver's Knee," *Los Angeles Times*, October 5, 1986, http://articles.latimes.com/1986-10-05/sports/sp-4447_1_red-sox.
3. Michael Martinez, "Angels Win in 11th to Take 3–1 Lead, *New York Times*, October 12, 1986, https://www.nytimes.com/1986/10/12/sports/angels-win-in-11th-to-take-3-1-lead.html.
4. Peter Golenbock, *Red Sox Nation: The Rich and Colorful History of the Boston Red Sox* (Chicago: Triumph Books, 2015), 419.
5. Ron Fimrite, "Good to the Very Last Out," *Sports Illustrated*, November 3, 1986, https://www.si.com/vault/1986/11/03/114291/good-to-the-very-last-out-the-mets-one-strike-from-defeat-staged-a-couple-of-remarkable-comebacks-to-deny-the-red-sox-their-first-world-series-in-68-years.
6. Ibid.
7. Ibid.

Chapter 17: Ups and Downs with Nomar and Mo

1. Elliott Teaford, "Indians Sweep Up Red Sox," October 7, 1995, *Los Angeles Times*, http://articles.latimes.com/1995-10-07/sports/sp-54313_1_red-sox.

2. Paul Doyle, "Finish Can't Save Kennedy from the End," *Hartford Courant*, October 1, 1996, https://www.courant.com/news/connecticut/hc-xpm-1996-10-01-9610010328 -story.html.

3. Ibid.

4. Ross Newhan, "They're Not Stopping Short of Saying He's Best," *Los Angeles Times*, August 24, 1997, http://articles.latimes.com/1997/aug/24/sports/sp-25664.

5. Jay Jaffe, "JAWS and the 2015 Hall of Fame Ballot: Nomar Garciaparra," *Sports Illustrated*, December 17, 2014, https://www.si.com/mlb/2014/12/17/jaws-2015-hall-of -fame-ballot-nomar-garciaparra.

Chapter 18: A Little Big Mistake

1. Lew Freedman, *The 50 Greatest Players in Boston Red Sox History* (Philadelphia: Camino Books, 2013), 79.

2. Bob Ryan, "Martinez's Sparkling Performance Loses No Luster a Day Later," *Boston Globe*, September 12, 1999, https://www.newspapers.com/newspage/441965571/.

3. Mark Hale, "Boston Battle Cry Has Red Sox Fans Ridin' High," *New York Post*, October 12, 2003, https://nypost.com/2003/10/12/boston-battle-cry-has-red-sox-fans -ridin-high/.

4. Peter Golenbock, *Red Sox Nation: The Rich and Colorful History of the Boston Red Sox* (Chicago: Triumph Books, 2015), 475.

5. Gordon Edes, "Hitless Wondering: In Crucial Spots, Garciaparra Isn't Hacking It," *Boston Globe*, October 15, 2003, http://archive.boston.com/sports/baseball/redsox/ articles/2003/10/15/hitless_wondering/.

6. Baseball Almanac, "Why Did You Keep Pedro In?", www.baseball-almanac.com/ box-scores/boxscore.php?boxid=200310160NYA.

Chapter 19: Big Papi and the Big Comeback

1. Rhett Bollinger, "Ryan Regrets Losing Ortiz," MLB.com, February 2, 2016, https:// www.mlb.com/news/terry-ryan-reflects-on-releasing-david-ortiz/c-163401054.

2. Phil Rogers, "Signing Ortiz Changed Red Sox's Course," MLB.com, November 18, 2015, https://www.mlb.com/news/louie-eljaua-helped-red-sox-sign-david-ortiz/ c-157612356.

3. Dan Shaughnessy, "The Dream Stays Alive: Sox Avert Sweep as Ortiz Homer Sinks N.Y. in 12th," *Boston Globe*, October 18, 2004, http://archive.boston.com/sports/ baseball/redsox/articles/2004/10/18/the_dream_stays_alive/.

4. Dan Shaughnessy, "A World Series Ticket: Sox Complete Comeback, Oust Yankees for AL Title," *Boston Globe*, October 21, 2004, http://archive.boston.com/sports/ baseball/redsox/articles/2004/10/21/a_world_series_party/.

5. Baseball Almanac, 2004 World Series, www.baseball-almanac.com/ws/yr2004ws .shtml.

6. Dan Lamothe, "Reminiscing: Remembering the 2004 Red Sox Victory Parade," Mass Live, February 13, 2007, http://blog.masslive.com/redsoxmonster/2007/02/ reminiscing_remembering_the_20.html.

CHAPTER 20: MANNY BEING MANNY

1. Joe Posnanski, "Make No Mistake, Manny Was a Genius at the Plate," MLB.com, January 19, 2018, http://wap.mlb.com/bos/news/article/20180117264796776/.

2. Bill Nowlin, Manny Ramirez, Society for American Baseball Research, https://sabr .org/bioproj/person/8d70b524.

3. ESPN. "Ramirez: Red Sox Losing ALCS Wouldn't Be 'End of the World,'" October 18, 2007, www.espn.com/mlb/playoffs2007/news/story?id=3068474.

4. Ibid.

5. Larry Fine, "Red Sox Sweep Colorado to Win World Series," *The Guardian*, October 29, 2007, https://www.theguardian.com/sport/2007/oct/30/ussport.

6. Peter Golenbock, *Red Sox Nation: The Rich and Colorful History of the Boston Red Sox* (Chicago: Triumph Books, 2015), 557.

7. Ken Rosenthal, "Manny Acknowledges Mistakes, Chases One Last Chance," Fox Sports, March 12, 2014, https://www.foxsports.com/mlb/story/manny-ramirez -acknowledging-mistakes-chases-one-last-chance-031214.

CHAPTER 21: CHICKEN AND CHAMPIONSHIPS

1. Bob Hohler, "Inside the Collapse," *Boston Globe*, October 12, 2011, http://archive .boston.com/sports/baseball/redsox/articles/2011/10/12/red_sox_unity_dedication_ dissolved_during_epic_late_season_collapse/.

2. Gordon Edes, "Terry Francona's Belated Revenge," ESPN, January 16, 2013, www .espn.com/boston/mlb/story/_/id/8848101/terry-francona-fires-back-boston-red-sox -owners.

3. C. Trent Rosecrans, "Don't Ask Bobby V. If He's 'Checked Out,' or He'll Punch You in the Mouth," CBS Sports, September 5, 2012, https://www.cbssports.com/mlb/news/ dont-ask-bobby-v-if-hes-checked-out-or-hell-punch-you-in-the-mouth/.

4. Dan Shaughnessy, "Red Sox Were a True Feel-Good Story for Boston," *Boston Globe*, October 31, 2013, https://www.bostonglobe.com/sports/2013/10/31/these-red-sox -were-true-feel-good-story-for-boston/egFbtJ4oBHMFF3CD7r1VOL/story.html.

5. Associated Press, "David Ortiz Says Goodbye to Fans After Red Sox Are Swept by Indians in ALDS," *New York Daily News*, October 11, 2016, https://www.nydailynews .com/sports/baseball/david-ortiz-goodbye-red-sox-swept-indians-article-1.2826006.

6. Ian Browne, "2018 Champs Stand Out as Greatest Sox Team," MLB.com, October 29, 2018, https://www.mlb.com/redsox/news/2018-world-series-champs-greatest-red -sox-team-c299908396.

CHAPTER 22: RED SOX NATION

1. Amy Bass, "We Believe: The Anatomy of Red Sox Nation," Chapter 9, in *Rooting for the Home Team: Sport, Community, and Identity*, edited by Daniel A. Nathan (Chicago: University of Illinois Press, 2013), 142, https://books.google.com/books?id=JILtwy9f6 NYC&pg=PA142&lpg=PA142&dq=Eckersley:+Ultimate+manic-depressive+fanbase& source=bl&ots=LDfsJQfeGJ&sig=ACfU3U2hnAsULRkDy-WaKBHKCsyk4Yzwkg& hl=en&sa=X&ved=2ahUKEwjx7YGG-prhAhXDz4MKHazdCf4Q6AEwAXoECAk

QAQ#v=onepage&q=Eckersley%3A%20Ultimate%20manic-depressive%20fanbase&f=false.

2. Stephanie Vosk, "Another Mystery of the Diamond, Explained At Last," *Boston Globe*, May 29, 2005, http://archive.boston.com/sports/baseball/redsox/articles/2005/05/29/another_mystery_of_the_diamond_explained_at_last/.

OTHER SOURCES

Associated Press. "Baseball Daily Report: Around the Majors: Boston's Clemens Goes on Disabled List." *Los Angeles Times*. https://www.latimes.com/archives/la-xpm -1993-06-22-sp-5645-story.html.

Associated Press. "Baseball; Dog Bites Hand That Pitches." *New York Times*, August 2, 1993. https://www.nytimes.com/1993/08/02/sports/baseball-dog-bites-hand -that-pitches.html.

Associated Press. "Sports People: Baseball; Red Sox Place Canseco on Disabled List." *New York Times*, May 18, 1995. https://www.nytimes.com/1995/05/18/sports/ sports-people-baseball-red-sox-place-canseco-on-disabled-list.html.

Bethune, Ian. "20-Game Winners in Red Sox History." Sox and Dawgs. https:// soxanddawgs.com/articles-redsox/20-game-winners-in-red-sox-history.html.

Boston's Pastime. "Red Sox Fans Love Their Dirty Water." https://www.bostonspastime .com/dirtywater.html.

Brown, Maury. "Breaking Down MLB's New 2017-21 Collective Bargaining Agreement." *Forbes*, November 30, 2016. https://www.forbes.com/sites/maurybrown/ 2016/11/30/breaking-down-mlbs-new-2017-21-collective-bargaining-agreement/ #681dac5411b9.

CBS Boston. "Dropkick Murphys to Lead Off Red Sox World Series Parade Through Boston," October 30, 2018. https://boston.cbslocal.com/2018/10/30/dropkick -murphys-red-sox-world-series-parade-boston-2018/.

Cobb, Nathan. "Sox Fan's Words Led to the Birth of a Nation." *Boston Globe*, September 26, 2005. http://archive.boston.com/sports/baseball/redsox/articles/2005/09/ 26/sox_fans_words_led_to_the_birth_of_a_nation/

Coffey, Alex. "Tom Seaver Announces His Retirement." National Baseball Hall of Fame. https://baseballhall.org/discover-more/stories/inside-pitch/tom-seaver -retirement.

Crouch, Ian. "Curt Schilling, Internet Embarrassment." *New Yorker*, April 21, 2016. https://www.newyorker.com/sports/sporting-scene/good-riddance-curt-schilling ?irclickid=X2fRrTxmDxyJRh0xTV1LXQupUklxhpTO8zuQQQ0&irgwc=1& source=affiliate_impactpmx_12f6tote_desktop_Viglink%20Primary&mbid= affiliate_impactpmx_12f6tote_desktop_Viglink%20Primary.

Dana Farber Cancer Institute. The Jimmy Fund. www.jimmyfund.org/about-us/boston -red-sox/history/.

Edes, Gordon. "In End, Deal Makes Sense." *Boston Globe*, August 5, 2004. http://archive.boston.com/sports/baseball/redsox/articles/2004/08/05/in_end_deal_made_sense/.

Fenway Fanatics. "Fenway Park History." www.fenwayfanatics.com/fenway-park/history/.

Games Kids Play. Piggy Move Up. http://www.gameskidsplay.net/games/ball_games/piggy_move_up.htm.

Gammons, Peter. "Peter Gammons: Carl Yastrzemski Is the Toughest player I've Ever Covered." Gammons Daily, August 21, 2017. www.gammonsdaily.com/peter-gammons-yaz-is-the-toughest-player-ive-ever-covered/.

Holmes, Dan. "Yankees Won Flag by Beating Red Sox on Final Sunday of Regular Season in 1949." Baseball Egg, July 24, 2012. http://baseballegg.com/2012/07/24/yankees-win-flag-by-beating-red-sox-on-final-sunday-of-regular-season/.

Murder, Craig. "Pedro Martinez Blanks Indians in Game 5 of ALDS." National Baseball Hall of Fame. https://baseballhall.org/discover/inside-pitch/pedro-martinez-blanks-indians-in-alds.

New England Historical Society. "Sunday Baseball Fails to Rescue the Boston Red Sox from the Cellar in 1929." www.newenglandhistoricalsociety.com/sunday-baseball-fails-to-rescue-the-boston-red-sox-from-the-cellar-in-1929/.

Schoenfield, David. "Best Seasons: Case for Carl Yastrzemski '67." ESPN, March 5, 2012. www.espn.com/blog/sweetspot/post/_/id/21380/best-seasons-case-for-carl-yastrzemski-67.

Shaughnessy, Dan. "And That's All: Red Sox Swept by Indians." *Boston Globe*, October 7, 1995. https://www.bostonglobe.com/sports/1995/10/07/and-that-all-red-sox-swept-indians/XcxPR3pcPekiq8YQsYl4dN/story.html.

Sporcle. "Can You Name the Red Sox HR leaders by Season?" https://www.sporcle.com/ames/Max_Power78/red-sox-hr-leaders-by-season.

Texas Sports: Longhorns Legends: Roger Clemens, February 11, 2005. https://texassports.com/news/2005/2/11/021105aaa_630.aspx.

Underhill, Nick. "The 10 Best 'Manny Being Manny' Moments." Mass Live, April 9, 2011. https://www.masslive.com/sports/2011/04/the_10_best_manny_being_manny.html.

United Press International. "Red Sox Send Tony Conigliaro to Angels in 6-Player Trade." *New York Times*, October 12, 1970. https://www.nytimes.com/1970/10/12/archives/red-sox-send-tony-conigliaro-to-angels-in-6-player-trade.html.

YouTube. "1975 World Series Gm 3: Fisk Gets Tangled Up with Armbrister." https://www.youtube.com/watch?v=dRw2_KvHcPk.

YouTube. "1986 World Series, Game 6: Red Sox @ Mets." https://www.youtube.com/watch?v=B0jV_kNs2p0.

YouTube. "2004 ALCS Gm 4: David Ortiz's Walk-Off Two Run Homer." https://www.youtube.com/watch?v=xYxSZJ9GZ-w.

YouTube. "2004 ALCS Gm 4: Roberts Sets Up, Scores Tying Run." https://www.youtube.com/watch?v=EMEylcp7E7s.

YouTube. "Roger Clemens Ejected from Playoff Game 1990." https://www.youtube
.com/watch?v=wtQoEA6GpPA.

Ziezima, Katie. "Two Yankees and Worker Are Charged in Fight." *New York Times*,
December 19, 2003. https://www.nytimes.com/2003/12/19/sports/baseball-2
-yankees-and-worker-are-charged-in-fight.html?mtrref=www.google.com&
gwh=A3F05950F88FDAFBEA9888DA83129C11&gwt=pay.